Cambridge Elements

Elements in Research Methods in Education
edited by
Sal Consoli
University of Edinburgh
Samantha Curle
University of Bath

HOW TO USE GENERATIVE AI IN EDUCATIONAL RESEARCH

Jasper Roe
Durham University

Shaftesbury Road, Cambridge CB2 8EA, United Kingdom

One Liberty Plaza, 20th Floor, New York, NY 10006, USA

477 Williamstown Road, Port Melbourne, VIC 3207, Australia

314–321, 3rd Floor, Plot 3, Splendor Forum, Jasola District Centre,
New Delhi – 110025, India

103 Penang Road, #05–06/07, Visioncrest Commercial, Singapore 238467

Cambridge University Press is part of Cambridge University Press & Assessment,
a department of the University of Cambridge.

We share the University's mission to contribute to society through the pursuit of
education, learning and research at the highest international levels of excellence.

www.cambridge.org
Information on this title: www.cambridge.org/9781009675321

DOI: 10.1017/9781009675338

© Jasper Roe 2025

This publication is in copyright. Subject to statutory exception and to the provisions of
relevant collective licensing agreements, no reproduction of any part may take place
without the written permission of Cambridge University Press & Assessment.

When citing this work, please include a reference to the DOI 10.1017/9781009675338

First published 2025

A catalogue record for this publication is available from the British Library

ISBN 978-1-009-67532-1 Hardback
ISBN 978-1-009-67534-5 Paperback
ISSN 3050-2861 (online)
ISSN 3050-2853 (print)

Cambridge University Press & Assessment has no responsibility for the persistence
or accuracy of URLs for external or third-party internet websites referred to in this
publication and does not guarantee that any content on such websites is, or will remain,
accurate or appropriate.

For EU product safety concerns, contact us at Calle de José Abascal, 56, 1°, 28003
Madrid, Spain, or email eugpsr@cambridge.org

How to Use Generative AI in Educational Research

Elements in Research Methods in Education

DOI: 10.1017/9781009675338
First published online: October 2025

Jasper Roe
Durham University

Author for correspondence: Jasper Roe, jasper.j.roe@durham.ac.uk

Abstract: Artificial Intelligence technologies have impacted our world in ways we could not have imagined a decade ago. Generative AI (GenAI), a powerful, complex and general use subset of AI has become available to the public in recent years. GenAI's effect on education, research, and academic practice is far-reaching and exciting, yet also deeply concerning. While GenAI has the potential to offer transformation in the practice of educational research, there are few resources which clarify why, when, and how these tools might be used ethically and sensitively. This Element introduces key areas of consideration for education researchers seeking to use GenAI, including examining the existing research, critically evaluating the benefits and risks of GenAI in educational research, and providing example use cases of good and bad practice.

Keywords: GenAI, education, research, Artificial Intelligence, educational studies

© Jasper Roe 2025

ISBNs: 9781009675321 (HB), 9781009675345 (PB), 9781009675338 (OC)
ISSNs: 3050-2861 (online), 3050-2853 (print)

Contents

A Note on Terminology	1
Introduction	1
Contextualising GenAI in Education	2
GenAI and Educational Research: Theoretical Foundations	5
The Potential Benefits of GenAI in Educational Research	11
The Risks of Using GenAI in Educational Research	14
How GenAI Shapes Educational Research Processes	24
Looking to the Future	43
Conclusion	45
How GenAI Was Used in This Element	45
A Checklist for GenAI Use in Educational Research	46
References	49

A Note on Terminology

A significant issue in the literature on Generative AI (GenAI) is the fact that the terminology is evolving at the same speed as technological capabilities. Especially in non-specialist computing literature, terms are often used synonymously or metonymically. For example, 'ChatGPT' is often used as a catch-all term for GenAI, and AI is used synonymously with GenAI. To adopt a clear approach, this text uses AI to describe the broad field of enquiry that describes systems capable of performing tasks that require human intelligence. Meanwhile, GenAI is defined as a subset of AI which can create (or generate) content, including text, images and video, sound, speech, music, software code, art, simulations, and synthetic data (IBM, 2024), and Large Language Models (LLMs) are a type of GenAI which primarily produce textual output. At times, the term 'AI' is used to reflect a broader range of technologies that may include GenAI. For the research field of AI in Education, the abbreviation AIED is used.

Introduction

Education as a field of study is poised to be transformed by the ever-greater deployment and widespread use of Artificial Intelligence (AI) technologies, and Generative Artificial Intelligence (GenAI) as a subtype of AI. Multibillion-dollar corporations such as OpenAI (the creator of ChatGPT) have begun to develop education-specific partnerships with leading higher education institutions, and government bodies are developing plans for widespread use of GenAI in K-12 institutions (GOV.UK, 2025). At the same time, the use of GenAI is dividing opinion among academics and polarising the landscape. Against this backdrop, this Element seeks to provide a comprehensive overview of the rationale behind using GenAI in educational research processes, the expected benefits to be reaped from such use, and the resultant risks of improper use. The Element systematically addresses the methodological dimensions of conducting research, including the relevance of theory, current trends in GenAI usage in differing fields of research, and specific applications in the areas of planning, data collection, analysis, reflexivity, and reporting.

The first section of this work (Contextualising GenAI in Education) involves a brief description and short history of the current context, explaining the origins of the current surge in interest around GenAI and clarifying key terminology, applications, and use cases. This is followed by exploring the role of educational theory and its relevance to GenAI-enabled research, and research investigating GenAI in educational processes. The next section explores the use of GenAI in broader, non-education-specific research processes, before critically examining the benefits, and associated risks, of uncritical GenAI use in educational research. After this, specific subsections address different dimensions of educational research methodologies, offering both practical guidance and a critical appraisal of the literature.

Contextualising GenAI in Education

AI generally refers to the proposition that computers are capable of thinking like humans, and this has been a topic in the scientific literature for more than half a century (Kaplan & Haenlein, 2019), although some suggest an origin back two centuries to the invention of the Jacquard loom or Charles Babbages' difference machine (Grzybowski et al., 2024). Ideas and philosophical discussions regarding something akin to AI can also be traced back to antiquity (Kaplan & Haenlein, 2019). Since the 1950s, AI has been described as going through cycles of abundant funding and interest, followed by periods of despondence and disinterest, commonly labelled as 'summers' and 'winters' (Floridi, 2020). It has been argued that the early to mid-2020s is in the midst of an 'AI bubble', or 'hype cycle', which could 'burst' and lead to another AI winter (Floridi, 2024). Although there is no predicting whether this will come to pass, it is hard to imagine that AI technologies will so quickly be abandoned, given the staggering investments being poured into AI corporations. It is predicted that this sum will approach 4 per cent of the GDP of the United States of America in the near future, and globally investments of billions are expected in 2025 (Goldman Sachs, 2024). In the United States of America, a new company named 'The Stargate Project' has committed to investing $500 billion into AI infrastructure (Hoskins & Rahman-Jones, 2025). AI is poised to define the coming decades and will greatly affect the social, political, economic, and environmental landscape – for better or worse.

The 2020s has been a tumultuous decade for education, with two major disruptive changes having taken place at the time of writing. The first of these is the COVID-19 pandemic. The need for physical distancing to slow viral transmission necessitated an overnight switch to online learning (Daniel, 2020) and accelerated the integration of technology into the learning experience, leading to greater uptake of AI and Virtual Reality technologies (Rashid & Yadav, 2020). New conversations about the validity and security of assessment and academic integrity came to the fore (Gamage et al., 2020; Roe, Perkins, Chonu et al., 2024; Turner et al., 2022) as did scrutiny over how technology perpetuates educational inequalities, especially in times of crisis (Stanistreet et al., 2020). Research examining the implications of the pandemic was prioritised in multiple fields, including education. While this monumental and tragic event was occurring, a new set of AI technologies was already under development.

Just as the pandemic began to ease and teachers and students returned to classrooms, news on AI started to trickle into public discourse. Two years on, the trickle has turned to a flood, and references to AI are everywhere, with almost every week seeing a slew of new headlines in the media on AI's perils and possibilities. But with this increased focus comes the potential for conflation, misinformation and disinformation, misunderstanding and confusion. So before describing the current state of GenAI and its applications in educational research, it must be clarified what we are talking about when we speak of AI.

Although there is no definitive 'start' to the current societal focus on AI, a watershed moment in the current AI boom occurred during 2017 and 2018, with the advent of Large Language Models (LLMs). In 2017, a new type of deep learning architecture known as a transformer was developed by researchers at Google. The transformer architecture, which uses a novel mechanism based on 'attention', was published in a now seminal paper by a number of Google employees in 2017, entitled '*Attention is all you need*' (Vaswani et al., 2017). The paper detailed the transformer architecture and demonstrated an application on English-to-German and English-to-French translation tasks. This was followed by the development of an LLM from Google AI, BERT (Bidirectional Encoder Representations from Transformers), using the transformer architecture (Devlin et al., 2019). Around this time, another company, OpenAI, combined transformer architecture with a technique known as unsupervised learning, removing the need for laborious human labelling of datasets with positive results (OpenAI, 2018). This was described in the paper that introduced the Generative Pretrained Transformer (GPT) (Radford, 2018). After several iterations, a public version (ChatGPT) based on the GPT 3.5 model was released to the public, followed in quick succession by numerous competitors from companies including Google and Anthropic. This new form of GenAI quickly gained notoriety for its impressive abilities at generating sophisticated, human-like text and demonstrating what seemed to be a sense of human-like intelligence. The conversational and interactional abilities of LLMs are so convincing that they can deceive users into believing that they are conscious (Shardlow & Przybyła, 2024). Current models can perform highly on a range of challenging benchmarks relating to mathematics and reasoning (Perrier & Bennett, 2024), or pass formal assessments such as those used for medical licensing (Gilson et al., 2023).

LLMs contain hundreds of billions of parameters (variables), are trained on huge amounts of textual data, and demonstrate capacities to understand natural language and complete or solve multiple tasks (Zhao et al., 2024). LLMs also demonstrate emergent properties, which suggests that scaling up their training and processing power may result in developing greater capabilities (Wei et al., 2022). LLMs are a type of GenAI technology that produces text, while GenAI more broadly includes multimodal outputs (such as text, images, audio, and more). Applications which once focused solely on textual output, for instance ChatGPT, have now become multimodal GenAI models. Recent multimodal innovations now gaining traction include NotebookLM, a product from Google that can summarise textual data in the form of an audiobook or podcast (Google, 2024a). Agentic models (such as Gemini 2) can assume the role of an agent and take action on behalf of the individual user (Pichai et al., 2024). While traditionally development of LLMs has been highly resource-intensive, new open-source models such as DeepSeek-R1 are gaining in notoriety for their ability to achieve outstanding results on formalised tests, after being developed at a far lower cost in comparison to other 'frontier models' (Hoskins & Rahman-Jones, 2025).

At the time of writing, publicly available GenAI models have been around for just a few years, demonstrating a staggering amount of development and improvement, with each week seemingly bringing new releases of improved models that perform greater and more complex tasks. In the midst of all this, scholarly and public discourse has polarised, and this can be seen in current news media. Research has shown that popular media, in the United Kingdom at least, tends to propagate the view that the emergence of a disruptive AI superintelligence is on the horizon, bringing about the destruction of life as we know it (see Roe & Perkins, 2023). On the other end of the spectrum are those who argue that AI promises economic and social liberation, with vast potential for solving social issues and improving efficiency (McMahon et al., 2025) or even 'saving the planet' (Herweijer, 2018). The impacts of AI are difficult to reduce to a binary set of 'risks' and 'benefits', given the wide-reaching and significant impacts that such technologies may have. Despite these complicated questions, in the academic space at least, it seems there is a growing consensus that educators must learn to adapt to a world in which some AI systems will become commonplace, and GenAI will be used to varying extents by students, teachers, administrators, and researchers. In other words, there is a recognition that the GenAI genie is already 'out of the bottle' (Zhgenti & Holmes, 2023), and thus, we must confront GenAI in education rather than turn away from it. While it is difficult not to talk about categories of 'risks' and 'benefits' to AI, it should be noted that these effects may be highly contextual and individually specific. For this reason, it is impossible to take a position that GenAI in education will be wholly bad, nor wholly good, and examining whether risks outweigh benefits or vice versa will not lead to satisfactory conclusions.

As a result of an increased recognition that AI is likely here to stay, scholarly research in the educational space has pivoted to the implications of the technologies, and the body of literature exploring GenAI is growing quickly. That said, despite a diverse range of GenAI applications now being available, and an intensely competitive landscape between billion-dollar corporations, many studies continue to focus solely on investigating the original public LLM tool – ChatGPT. This focus is so intense that ChatGPT is seemingly close to becoming a proprietary eponym, or shorthand, for GenAI in general. Over the short time that academic research has been ongoing, some debates have seemingly been settled – for example, whether ChatGPT can be labelled an author on scientific papers (it seems it cannot) (Goto & Katanoda, 2023) yet new debates have arisen, such as whether GenAI is a viable tool for data analysis. One of the key challenges in unpacking these debates is that quality research takes a significant investment of time and effort, as does peer review. Thus, by the time researchers can dig into detail and understand the capabilities and impacts of a GenAI model, a newer version has been released. On the other hand, most software tools are updated on a continuous basis, suggesting that this is not a problem unique to GenAI. Nevertheless, the literature base has developed to the point that publication of systematic reviews is now becoming viable (Deng et al., 2025; Wang et al., 2024), thus giving a clearer sense of exactly what the impacts of GenAI may be in some aspects of educational practice.

GenAI and Educational Research: Theoretical Foundations

Ontological and epistemological considerations represent an area that requires careful reflection when engaging with GenAI in educational research. For example, using GenAI tools to assist with the qualitative analysis of data may be in step with a constructivist paradigm, as GenAI models can extract themes or topics from data using pattern recognition. For researchers engaged in an interpretivist paradigm, GenAI will likely not be viewed as able to deeply interpret the depths of human experience, thus the application of GenAI to engage with data analysis is limited. For those conducting research from a positivist approach, the use of GenAI equally challenges notions of objective truth, given that outputs stated as 'fact' inherently represent biases from the data on which they were trained. This aspect feeds into the political and ideological forces that contribute to shaping the GenAI tools that a researcher may have at their disposal. As such, these first questions of epistemology, ontology, and guiding theory are a prerequisite for consideration before tackling the more practical use cases of GenAI in educational research.

Theory has long been recognised as essential for driving quality educational research (Suppes, 1974). When conducting research on the use of GenAI in education, or using GenAI to assist with research, there are a great many educational and learning theories which can be considered. Thus, it is relevant to start with a discussion of theoretical approaches. In a scoping review, Wang et al.'s (2024b) systematic literature review of AI in education found that 45 different theoretical approaches were used to scaffold research projects across 2,223 papers. It is not within the scope of this piece to give a comprehensive assessment of these. However, it is possible to draw on some of the ways in which common educational theories may resonate with GenAI in education. For these purposes, the major theoretical approaches of connectivism, social constructivism, and critical pedagogy are appropriate.

Connectivism

Through the lens of connectivism, knowledge emerges from the interconnections between different entities, including people, tools or nodes of information, and so as one entity changes, the connected entities may also change, giving rise to a connected network of ideas (Downes, 2022). According to Siemens (2018, p. 5) principles of connectivism include:

- Learning and knowledge rest in a diversity of opinions.
- Learning is a process of connecting specialised nodes or information sources.
- Learning may reside in non-human appliances.
- The capacity to know more is more critical than what is currently known.
- Nurturing and maintaining connections is necessary to facilitate continual learning.
- The ability to see connections between fields, ideas, and concepts is a core skill.
- Currency (in this context meaning up-to-date knowledge) is the goal of connectivist learning activities.
- Decision-making is a learning process: choosing what to learn and determining the meaning of incoming information is viewed through the lens of a shifting reality. The 'right' answer today may become outdated tomorrow due to changes in the information landscape.

Under connectivism, the fact that knowledge can reside in non-human appliances and can be developed through interaction with technology reflects a clear alignment with GenAI tools. Connectivism is highly relevant to educational research with GenAI as this theory may be operationalised to suggest that LLMs and other GenAI tools operate as new nodes in a learning network. Following this, GenAI models can therefore influence development by providing specialised resources, highlighting areas of confluence in multiple fields, or contributing new interpretations of data. For example, if a doctoral student were to use a GenAI-integrated summarisation tool for literature such as Elicit.AI, this could be interpreted as extending the network of understanding beyond a traditional set of scholarly databases. By examining how learners engage with and use GenAI content, researchers may be able to apply connectivism as the theoretical frame for research. Although there is a relative lack of studies exploring GenAI through a connectivist lens, Liang and Bai (2024) note that GenAI may be able to develop new dialogic spaces for connectivist-relevant aspects of learning. This is due to the fact that using these tools, for instance a GenAI chatbot, could support knowledge connectivity and expand information networks, while connecting learners to research and topics relevant to their field of study. In sum, connectivism is a promising theoretical approach for underpinning studies that explore GenAI in educational contexts, or in investigating how GenAI can be used in educational research or further study.

Critical Pedagogy

There are excellent reasons that critical pedagogy (Freire, 2000) is a suitable theoretical orientation for examining GenAI in education and educational research. Core principles of critical pedagogy include:

- A commitment to liberating oppressed populations.
- Supports creating emancipatory practices in learning environments such as schools.
- Critically examines systems of power in educational contexts.
- Draws on multiple diverse intellectual traditions that focus on social justice.
- Focuses on developing critical awareness in teachers and students.
- Aims to foster social change through teaching and learning (Darder et al., 2023).

These principles are relevant to GenAI, as the companies responsible for model development are often multibillion-dollar corporations located in the Global North, embedded in relations of capital and politics, which may ultimately perpetuate digital divides (Zhgenti & Holmes, 2023). Some authors have begun to apply this theoretical and methodological framework. Roe and Perkins (2024b) conducted a scoping review of literature on GenAI and student agency with attention to Critical Digital Pedagogy principles, including access, equity, and control, finding that GenAI may negatively impact learner agency, while Nyaaba et al. (2024a) examined digital neocolonialism as a consequence of GenAI, positing that tools such as ChatGPT may exhibit pedagogy control. This demonstration was achieved by generating a lesson plan through the GenAI model and noting that the lesson plan implicitly assumed individual student ownership of tablet computers, with content more suited to students in wealthier contexts and in the Global North.

Freire (2000) called for educational approaches that foster the development of critical consciousness and enable the perception of inequitable patterns in society (Warr, 2024), criticising the 'banking concept' of education, wherein students are passive vessels in which information is deposited, thus perpetuating oppressive structures. Educational researchers interested in understanding and using GenAI may wish to pay attention to this theory as LLMs and GenAI models may perpetuate dominant Western or Eurocentric cultural narratives, which may promote 'cultural invasion' (Freire, 2000) – that is to say, encouraging learners to fit existing structures rather than prompting them to question inequality. GenAI may thus become a site for social struggle. Whether seeking a framework by which to investigate issues relating to GenAI use and inequality and criticality, or whether seeking to use GenAI to assist with research tasks, educational researchers would be well-advised to consider the relevance of critical pedagogical approaches. The applicability of critical pedagogy in understanding and exploring GenAI in education is promising, and is demonstrated by the emerging research which uses this theoretical approach (Alm & Watanabe, 2023; Asmawi & Alam, 2024; Baskara, 2024; Sarı et al., 2024).

Social Constructivism

Core principles of social constructivism in the Vygotskian tradition include:

- Learner construction of knowledge is part of a process of social interaction and interpretation (Adams, 2006; Vygotsky, 1962).
- Learning and knowledge is actively structured rather than passively absorbed (Liu & Matthews, 2005).
- Social interactions influence cognitive development processes, which indicate that collaborative learning is highly beneficial (Richter et al., 2024).
- Learning is undertaken through interpretation rather than transmission (Cobern, 1993).

Constructivism is an influential theory in educational research and is especially suited to exploring the use of GenAI in learning and research writing processes. In Wang et al.'s (2024b) systematic literature review on AI in education, constructivism was among the most common theories utilised in research studies. In order to design learning from a constructivist perspective, active engagement and student-centred learning are key (Honig, 2024). One of the major benefits of GenAI tools is that they enable an interactive dialogue, thus supporting the ability for learners to query, question, discuss, and reformulate and reinterpret knowledge – rather than be given information to memorise as passive learners. On the other hand, it could be argued that as GenAI models are not social beings, they cannot be viewed from a constructivist perspective in this way. Interestingly, Honig's (2024) research demonstrates that, in fact, learners using a GenAI tutor preferred non-constructivist activities to constructivist activities, which means that further research involving constructivist approaches to learning would be valuable to inform these findings. Grubaugh et al. (2023) note that AI and constructivism share common ground, as intelligent tutoring systems can adaptively respond to students, thus focusing on active knowledge building and adaptive support, and Honig (2024) argues that GenAI offers the opportunity to better integrate constructivist learning designs into education. In summary, social constructivism states that knowledge construction takes place through collaborative, contextualised interpretation rather than passive transmission (Liu & Matthews, 2005). In the context of GenAI, tools such as GPT-based systems lend themselves to interactive, dialogic learning experiences that resonate with constructivist principles, which then allow learners to query, question, and co-construct meaning (Honig, 2024). Consequently, for educational researchers interested in exploring GenAI through a social constructivist theoretical approach, there are significant areas of correspondence that may be explored.

The theoretical approaches of connectivism, critical pedagogy, and social constructivism each highlight a different dimension of how GenAI might shape contemporary education and are thus relevant to educational researchers. Connectivism frames learning as the growth of diverse networks of information and connections, while critical pedagogy draws attention to cultural biases, power imbalances, and addressing inequities and inequalities, and social constructivism underscores the active nature of knowledge building and the importance of critical engagement with AI-generated content. Although these are not the only theories relevant to GenAI in educational studies, taken together, they can inform the design, implementation, and interpretation of GenAI based interventions in an educational context or research design methodology. Furthermore, such approaches may be combined – a blended theoretical approach, for example, could consider analysing the networking of learning behaviours through GenAI tools (connectivism) while simultaneously addressing power relations and inclusivity in the classroom (critical pedagogy), while also reflecting on collaborative sense-making (constructivism). The aim of this section however is not to propose specific methodologies nor dictate a research agenda, but to stress the role and importance of using theory in educational research regarding GenAI, rather than undertaking supposedly atheoretical studies into how GenAI is used in educational environments or in research processes. In the following section, a thorough analysis of both the benefits and risks of GenAI in educational research is given, providing a clearer set of practical considerations to consider in addition to theoretical perspectives.

To understand the potential implications for research using GenAI, it is also helpful to have a grasp of the direction of the field, and what educational researchers are focusing on when it comes to GenAI. For example, today's multimodal GenAI models are not limited to text, and outputs can include multiple forms of media, extending to music, art, and synthetic data (IBM, 2024) or even emulating a person's likeness (Roe, Perkins, & Furze, 2024). However, despite these burgeoning multimodal applications coming to light, much of the extant literature to date explores the use of text-based chatbots and their applications in educational activities – for example, supporting learners through tutoring (Limo et al., 2023) or providing feedback (George, 2023) and assisting with lesson planning (van den Berg & du Plessis, 2023). It is important to be aware that using GenAI in educational research then, does not necessarily mean that only textual output is being considered.

Institutions and educators have had limited time to understand these technologies (Bozkurt, 2023). There may still be a significant lack of awareness on how they can be used in research, although evidence suggests there is a move towards permissibility in line with ethical principles among institutions and academic publishers (Jin et al., 2025; Perkins & Roe, 2024a, 2024b). The rationale for such acceptance is that there are many potential benefits to be reaped from the use of GenAI in academic research (Rudolph et al., 2024), and there is evidence that such tools are viewed positively by academics (Bringula, 2025). Moreover, data suggests that many researchers are already engaging GenAI to assist with their work in multiple fields. A 2023 study of 1,600 scientists revealed that 30 per cent of respondents used GenAI to compose academic papers (Singh Chawla, 2024), while a study presented at the 2024 NeurIPS conference highlighted that over 70 per cent of authors found LLMs helpful for refining their manuscripts during the peer review process (Ginde, 2024). Gray (2024) estimated that in 2023, over 60,000 scientific papers were LLM-assisted, slightly over 1 per cent of all articles published, while Picazo-Sanchez and Ortiz-Martin (2024) found that between December 2022 and February 2023, ChatGPT played a role in 10 per cent of abstracts ($N = 45,000$) across 317 journals. There is limited research investigating the different types of AI use found in these manuscripts. From a research integrity standpoint, there is evidence that AI-assisted papers written by third parties (e.g., papermills) are becoming popular and more widely available (Gaumann & Veale, 2024). This suggests that a subsection of these papers which are LLM-assisted could be attributable to papermills.

Usage of GenAI may also extend to the peer review process, and not just composition of original research works, with Delios et al. (2024) noting that AI-generated peer reviews are now likely being created, with some 'telltale adjectives' produced by ChatGPT have increased in some studies on peer review reports (Singh Chawla, 2024). Although there is little information on the demographics of those using GenAI in research, one large scale study of researchers in Danish universities ($N = 2,534$) evaluating thirty-two use cases found that junior scholars tend to use GenAI more than senior researchers, and all participants viewed using GenAI for language and editing positively, while perceptions of more complex tasks such as research design were more variable and nuanced (Bjelobaba et al., 2024).

Although GenAI is a 'double-edged sword' (Delios et al., 2024; Tang, 2024), the growing prevalence of usage by researchers suggests many view the benefits as outweighing the risks. It seems that the greatest benefit is that fundamentally, producing scientific research can be made easier, and some of the 'legwork' can be offloaded to these tools, including potentially recognising and reducing human error (Burger et al., 2023). It cannot be denied that producing educational research (much like any form of research) is difficult, time-consuming, and requires a combination of multiple different skillsets, and this is why prior to GenAI, many tools have been developed to help streamline the process (e.g., citation managers, software packages, or even outsourced external editing and proofreading services). Consequently, the major perceived benefits of GenAI in educational research appear to be improving efficiency, stimulating creativity, democratising research, and offering an opportunity for innovation. Each of these benefits is explained in detail next.

The Potential Benefits of GenAI in Educational Research

Efficiency and Productivity

GenAI may accelerate research productivity and thus benefit scientific advances in multiple fields (Al-Zahrani, 2024), as well as helping to reduce stress and improve time management for academics (Bin-Nashwan et al., 2023). Some authors even go so far as to claim that research tasks that previously took months can now be completed in seconds (Han et al., 2024). However, whether these cases lead to improved research quality, or merely quicker research output, has yet to be empirically validated, and promises to produce endless, high-quality research in short periods of time should be treated critically. One of the more prominent use cases for GenAI models such as ChatGPT is in the final, writing up stages of a research project. Regardless of field, the process of putting together coherent text, conducting literature reviews, and assembling the findings into a publishable document is a difficult undertaking. The fact that GenAI tools can instantaneously evaluate the coherence of a piece of text, identify errors and areas for improvement, and even provide exemplar text is therefore a benefit. The timesaving and efficiency provided by using GenAI tools in this stage of research is therefore highly appealing in a competitive, marketized academic landscape which often relies on publication metrics to quantify success. For research students especially, who may struggle with composing academic work, GenAI may be used to assist with polishing writing, as well as providing instruction and guidance on conducting scholarship (Chan & Colloton, 2024).

Stimulating Creativity

In educational research, creativity is often required in conceptualising a study, generating a question, or identifying a gap in the literature. This process can be challenging. Peres et al. (2023) highlight that a potential use of GenAI tools is to assist in creative thought and identify promising research questions, and Ansari et al. (2024) note that ChatGPT can be of assistance in formulating hypotheses, or justifying how significant a research project is. Often, having a 'critical friend' or partner to discuss ideas or brainstorm with can be helpful for the creative aspect of the research process, and GenAI tools may be able to provide this sounding board for testing out and considering ideas at the initial conception stage of research. At a more affective level, GenAI tools may be able to provide critical encouragement, ask probing questions, or help examine the feasibility of a research task – this can help researchers who are uncertain on how to begin their work. Breaking down a task into a step of achievable goals, suggesting a calendar and providing a template for accountability and progress may also help turn a creative idea into a reality.

Democratisation

A common concern regarding GenAI is its ability to compound educational inequalities (Zhgenti & Holmes, 2023). However, the inverse may also be true in some areas of educational research, as GenAI tools may contribute to mitigating entrenched inequalities. One example is eliminating the need for 'gift authorships'. Barros et al. (2023) contend that such authorships may be given to academics who provide only minor linguistic or stylistic edits. Given that GenAI tools can fulfil this role, there is the potential for this ethically dubious practice to be reduced, as rather than asking for the support of another, this function can now be fulfilled by technology. This argument of linguistic democratisation is tenable given that the dominant language of scientific publication is English, and that there is strong evidence that non-native English speakers face an uphill battle when participating in science. Amano et al. (2023) note that early career researchers who are not first-language English speakers expend more effort in reading and writing, preparing presentations, and disseminating research, while language barriers may also affect participation in international conferences. Although machine translation is not a new technology, the ease of access and advanced capabilities of GenAI for translating, editing, summarising, and improving overall written clarity may help to reduce this unequal balance and help minimise the linguistic challenges educational researchers face in widely disseminating their findings (Peres et al., 2023), and so GenAI could create a more inclusive and accessible publication landscape. This could be one explanation why a study of GenAI acknowledgements in academic publications found that two-thirds of corresponding authors were from non-English-speaking countries (Kousha, 2024).

Novel methods of dissemination may also help researchers who have previously been unable to afford professional assistance, or those without the resources to disseminate work to a non-specialist audience. For example, multimodal tools such as NotebookLM could enable researchers to turn their findings into accessible formats such as podcasts or audiobooks, thus generating wide community engagement. In seeking greater impact, researchers may be able to generate visualisations or short videos describing research results, or develop higher quality diagrams or bitesize textual summaries that are adaptable to different languages and styles. GenAI models could be used to assist researchers with forming plans for dissemination and generating broader impact, thus contributing to lessening the inequality between researchers who have and do not have access to greater resources and funding.

Innovation

Just as GenAI gives us new tools with which to conduct certain aspects of research, including planning, analysis, and writing and dissemination of results, GenAI is also a subject for innovative study and scholarship itself. The study of GenAI outputs allows researchers to gain new insights into different kinds of phenomena. For example, Omena et al. (2024) contend that by examining biased outputs in image generation models, new insights can be generated into social dynamics, casting light on existing social equity issues. This could be a subject of particular interest to researchers in the sociology of education. Furthermore, GenAI has reinvigorated not only computational fields of study, but also enabled the exploration of new possibilities in educational arenas. In this case, GenAI could be said to have stimulated a reflection on common issues in educational practice, such as teaching, learning and assessment, leading to new innovations. Finally, augmenting human reflection with computational insights provides opportunities for activities such as hybrid data analysis, which may lead to more creative, or more insightful analysis of data (Barros et al., 2023). Ultimately, this benefit is more geared towards the assertion that GenAI is a new, powerful set of technologies which will have significant impacts on education and offer approaches for innovation. Consequently, there is a duty and imperative to use and explore the tools as researchers ourselves.

In sum, regardless of the concern over whether GenAI is a bubble that is about to burst, a fad which will fade, or a technology that has already reached its potential, it must be acknowledged that there are benefits to be found in its use in research, as borne out by the rapid uptake in its use in the literature. When the risk and benefit profile is favourable is a different matter. In the following, the sizeable overall challenges related to using GenAI in educational research are discussed.

The Risks of Using GenAI in Educational Research

The benefits of GenAI in educational research are compelling. The possibility of creating new, innovative ways of conducting educational research, and doing so with greater speed and efficiency, is no doubt exciting. On the other hand, no existing data has validated that educational research (or any research) published using GenAI has improved the overall quality of outputs. This is concerning, given that there are serious risks associated with GenAI models, including the tendency for fabrication of outputs, a lack of transparency, replicability, and reliability, academic integrity concerns, data privacy, and environmental and cultural impacts.

Hallucinations

Perhaps the largest concern regarding the use of GenAI in educational research is 'hallucinations', a feature which has resulted in ChatGPT being labelled as both 'bullshit' (Hicks et al., 2024) and potentially a 'bullshit spewer' (Rudolph et al., 2023a). 'Hallucinations' is an unnecessarily anthropomorphic and potentially misleading term (Hicks et al., 2024; Zhgenti & Holmes, 2023), yet one which has become commonplace in the literature and in public discourse. Hallucinations are factually inaccurate, made-up, or fabricated outputs (Zhgenti & Holmes, 2023) produced by GenAI models with no awareness of the limits of their own knowledge (Huang et al., 2024). One reason for the common argument that LLMs and GenAI chatbots are merely 'stochastic parrots' (a phrase used in Bender et al.'s (2021) controversial paper) is the prevalence of hallucinations in the content they produce. This term suggests that GenAI tools merely 'cut and paste' or reassemble content from training data, and have no understanding of their output (Arkoudas, 2023). It has been argued that no matter the advancement or power of the computer involved, there exists an 'unbridgeable gap' between computing machines and human-level reasoning (Bishop, 2021). Although there is significant debate over whether this is the case, Arkoudas (2023) argues that the term 'stochastic parrots' is no longer applicable given the huge advances in multiple capabilities that GenAI tools have become capable of in the newest iterations (e.g., OpenAI's o1 model which can spend greater time 'thinking'), although this has not solved the hallucination issue.

Whether hallucinations can be mitigated, reduced, or eliminated is an open question, yet one that will determine the viability of these models in multiple domains, including educational research. One posited cause of hallucinations is the mixture of factual and counterfactual or inaccurate content in training data (Banh & Strobel, 2023), but others claim that conversely, hallucinations are fundamental characteristic of LLMs that go beyond training data (Yao et al., 2024), or that statistical analyses effectively demonstrates that hallucinations are an inevitable feature of LLMs which are inherent in the architecture, thus are not solvable (Banerjee et al., 2024). In terms of mitigating hallucinations, focus is now being given to techniques such as retrieval-augmented generation (RAG) to mitigate fabrications or misstatements and improve accuracy (Huang et al., 2024), and Microsoft has claimed that new features can identify and correct misleading or incorrect GenAI outputs (Chadwick, 2024). Despite this potential progress, Delios et al. (2024) argue that even if hallucinations become less frequent, it is unlikely that they will ever reduce to zero.

If solving hallucinations will not be a quick fix (if it is possible at all), educational researchers then need to consider what this means for potential use cases in scholarly work. One of the key areas in which hallucinations present themselves when using GenAI to assist with research is in the fabrication of false references, quotes, or publications. It has been documented that GenAI models such as ChatGPT produce false, non-existent citations and references to academic material, often resembling real publications or mimicking titles (Alser & Waisberg, 2023; Day, 2023), and anecdotally, searching for falsified references is a common tactic for identifying AI-generated material. One of the key proposed benefits of GenAI use in educational research, especially in writing up, in literature reviews, or analysis of data, is time-saving and efficiency. Hallucinations pose a fundamental challenge to this benefit being realised, if the output cannot be trusted to be fully accurate, then there is no time saved at all – on the contrary, the researcher is left with two choices. The first of these is to accept the risk that there may be fundamental, significant errors in the output that they have produced and use it anyway to save time. The second is to meticulously inspect and validate the GenAI-generated content of the research project, which may take just as much time as if the tools were not used in the first place.

Further to this, if the researcher blindly trusts in the content generated by a GenAI model, and should it be published and make its way past editors and peer reviewers, then the potential impacts are manifold. While competent peer reviewers should be able to identify falsified references or incorrect quotes, there is no guarantee that some will not slip past a reviewer's attention, especially if they are highly convincing hallucinated output. In the worst case, published educational research that has falsified or hallucinated references, data, or conclusions may be used to inform policies and practices in schools, allocate funding, and guide law and governance. Incorrect information here may lead to significant negative societal consequences, and the responsibility rests firmly with the researcher. For this reason, hallucinations, or fabricated, incorrect factual output is one of the most severe impediments to GenAI use in educational research. In the unlikely event that a completely hallucination-free GenAI model comes to the fore, then the potential risk-benefit profile of use in research may significantly shift, but as of now, this remains a central obstacle.

Replicability, Reliability and Quality

Outputs from GenAI models vary in content, even when using the same prompts multiple times. GenAI is referred to as a 'black box' frequently (Bearman & Ajjawi, 2023; Roe et al., 2024; Zhgenti & Holmes, 2023), given its lack of transparency in producing these variable outputs. GenAI developers do not transparently communicate how models are trained, or how and why they generate certain responses (Delios et al., 2024; Zhgenti & Holmes, 2023). From an educational research perspective, this is consequential. While educational research may not always rely on replicability (e.g., in ethnographic or phenomenology-oriented studies), the use of GenAI tools in specific settings, such as in statistical analysis of public datasets, may compromise replicability. Further to this, if inaccurate, or poor-quality analyses using GenAI are published, this may lead to downstream effects as these analyses may form future training data for AI models. This could cause a ripple effect, impacting the quality of future scientific analysis using GenAI models.

In review studies, such as systematic or scoping reviews, using GenAI tools for search processes will also potentially lead to non-replicability. While a search of an established database (such as SCOPUS) with clear exclusion and inclusion criteria should theoretically be replicable, conducting that same search with a GenAI tool may give a different set of studies each time, and as with the hallucinations challenge above, many of these sources may be fabricated. Moreover, one feature of current GenAI models is that very minor alterations to prompts can drastically change outputs, meaning that a standard of replicability or reliability is not achievable (Dowling & Lucey, 2023). Again, as with hallucinations, this does not mean that GenAI tools are unusable in educational research, but it does call for serious consideration of the risk and benefit profile. In some cases, this may mean simply that a disclaimer that the study may not be replicable is needed – but this could undermine trust in the research and invalidate the significance of the results, or the validity of the study.

Further issues arise when it comes to asking for guidance on methodological decisions, for instance what data analysis tool to use, the sampling technique, or a suggested sample size – while these are tasks that GenAI tools may assist in, and will provide instantaneous and confident answers, there is no way to clearly validate what they are saying is correct, as the process behind arriving at the answer is not given. In this case, the lack of transparency must usually be validated by the user externally. For instance, if a user asks a GenAI model to produce a research plan including a sample size, survey questions, suggested theoretical framework and analytical tools, the result may sound highly convincing – but there is nothing to clearly evidence that this has been based on a coherent and up-to-date investigation into best practice, and this means that the user cannot have full confidence in the suggestions. This is one reason that there is now a focus on the development of 'explainable AI', in which intelligent systems describe how results or outputs were arrived at (Xu et al., 2019). On the other hand, Turobov et al. (2024) point out that in some ways, human cognition may also be considered a black box, in that the decision-making process behind human action and behaviour is similarly non-transparent. Despite this philosophical argument, adhering to principles of transparency where possible is desirable for educational research, and so this is a challenge that educational researchers must consider.

Ethics, Research, and Academic Integrity

One of the most important consequences of GenAI's capabilities in producing high-quality, detailed and human-like text is the possibility for enabling academic integrity violations. Academic integrity can broadly be defined in this context as the focus on 'values, behaviour, and conduct of academics in all aspects of their practice' (Macfarlane et al., 2014, p. 1), and abiding by values of honesty, trust, fairness, respect and responsibility (TEQSA, 2022). In terms of violations from a research perspective, the principles of trust and honesty may be violated when GenAI tools are used to produce content which is then passed off as the author's own work.

The misuse of GenAI tools in ways that violate these values may result in plagiarism or misconduct accusations for students or researchers (Cotton et al., 2024; Perkins, 2023). The effort for educators and stakeholders to find technological means of identifying these uses has become part of an 'arms race' of technological developments to counter academic integrity violations (Eaton, 2022; Roe & Perkins, 2022). As part of this arms race, AI-generated text detection technologies have been implemented to attempt to identify undeclared or non-transparent usage in both journal article submissions and through assessment platforms at educational institutions. These efforts are largely misguided, given that research shows that these detectors are often wrong, easily fooled, and insufficient for detecting modern GenAI output (Perkins, Roe, et al., 2024; Weber-Wulff et al., 2023) and commonly produce false positives (Dalalah & Dalalah, 2023). These false accusations can cause serious harm to students' academic journeys (Roe et al., 2024) and may disproportionately affect non-native English speakers (Liang et al., 2023), and the same can be said for authors publishing in scholarly journals.

While it seems technological solutions are not accurate for protecting academic integrity, it is understandable for researchers, journal editors, and reviewers to now be on alert. Barros et al. (2023) point out that there is a proliferation of poor-quality and irrelevant manuscripts submitted to scholarly journals, in which GenAI tools like ChatGPT have been used to generate huge portions of work with little effort on behalf of the authors, thus violating principles of responsibility, transparency and honesty. AI-generated papers may also seem convincing at first read yet be factually inaccurate (Ariyaratne et al., 2023). Barros et al. (2023) attribute part of this to the 'publish or perish' culture, which places value on publication numbers. Simultaneously, it is likely that GenAI tools are being used to develop peer reviews of articles (Hosseini & Horbach, 2023). This may lead to the strange case of GenAI-produced manuscripts being reviewed by GenAI tools themselves, compromising the research process.

More obvious uses of GenAI in ways that could violate academic integrity principles are visible when there are 'footprints' of usage (Tang & Eaton, 2024), identification of which does not require the use of detection software. These 'footprints' are phrases that are common to GenAI models, which appear in peer-reviewed scholarly publications, for example '*As an AI language model ...* ' (Tang & Eaton, 2024), and so are identifiable by a reader. A website dedicated to cataloguing these cases documents 668 reported suspected cases at the time of writing (Academ-AI, 2024). The Academ-AI website offers examples of published work, in high-quality outlets indexed in leading academic databases wherein common GenAI phraseology such as '*Certainly, here are some ...* ' and '*as of my last knowledge update ...* '. Of the 668 reported suspected cases, 69 appear in the field of educational sciences. Such footprints should not be considered as an automatic violation of academic integrity values, as long as transparent use of GenAI tools was reported at the time of publication. This does not mean to say that it is acceptable practice, but such cases can indicate poor quality of work or a lack of attention to detail, rather than wilful disguising of authorship.

However, it is not just the failure to disclose the use of GenAI in research writing and processes that can amount to a failing to uphold academic integrity. There are also broader questions about copyright and ethicality of using others' intellectual property to train models, and whether phrases used are word-for-word reproductions, as has been noted to occur with ChatGPT (Alser & Waisberg, 2023). In considering the academic integrity implications of GenAI in research, however, we can go beyond just the textual level. Although plagiarism and failure to submit authentically human-generated work is one aspect worthy of consideration, the possibility for GenAI to be involved in faking multimodal research data is also important. GenAI tools may be used for the creation of synthetic media that could be used as fabricated or falsified research data (Kiley, 2024).

Over two years, the narrative on academic integrity in universities and schools has shifted, with many institutions now adopting frameworks that permit judicious use of AI tools (Bridgeman et al., 2024; Furze et al., 2024; Perkins, Furze, et al., 2024) in line with values of academic integrity. A similar situation has played out in the research sphere, with many publishers and funding bodies for research grants may now allowing certain aspects of GenAI use, as long as it is clear and transparently declared with authors taking full responsibility for the output. Common features in scholarly publishing include requiring a declaration of AI use and rejecting the listing of tools as co-authors (Kiley, 2024). To an extent, this mirrors what Eaton (2023) calls part of an era of postplagiarism, in which humans may be able to retain control over written output, but also offload or give control to AI tools where desired, while at the same time retaining overall accountability and responsibility for the truthfulness and accuracy of the output.

Positionality and Reflexivity

A further issue that must be considered relates to the positionality of the researcher. In this case, positionality refers to the stance of the researcher in reference to the context of the research participants (Coghlan & Brydon-Miller, 2014), including how they are viewed by themselves and others (Ozano &

Khatri, 2018). Positionality affects every stage of the research, including at the very earliest stages of ideation or planning the process (Coghlan & Brydon-Miller, 2014). Positionality matters as what is viewed as a 'research problem' invariably relates to those with the power to access and construct new knowledge (Ríos & Patel, 2023). Using GenAI models in educational research must be considered with regard to this aspect of investigation, as GenAI models can be highly culturally biased and may impose Western worldviews and norms on non-Western societies (Nyaaba et al., 2024b) or promote ethnocentric viewpoints (Hurley, 2024). Consequently, researchers must consider to what extent the use of GenAI affects their positionality and might influence the researcher–participant relationship. To give an example, if a researcher employs a GenAI model to interpret transcripts from an interviewer, the algorithmic nature of the model may overlook less visible forms of data, less common linguistic expressions, or may otherwise privilege certain modes of knowledge and existence. To counteract this, researchers must proactively engage with this challenge. Methods for dealing with such issues include reflexive journalling, in which the researcher consistently interrogates and considers the influence of their own assumptions, cultural context, and positionality. Further to this, researchers must communicate transparently about not only how GenAI will be used, but also how it may shape findings and be influenced by the potential biases and limitations in these tools. By practicing reflexivity in the research process, and accepting the fact that educational research can never be value-free (Basit, 2013), this challenge can be better addressed.

Data Privacy

Educational research often involves handling sensitive data. Such data could contain identifying information of individuals or private information that an individual has consented to be shared with the researcher only. Data may include personal beliefs, attitudes towards an educational institution or government body, or reports on children's behaviour and achievement in the classroom. Given the nature of this data, information privacy and secure handling of data is of utmost importance in educational research. A worrying situation in the use of GenAI tools then, is sharing of such sensitive data with third-party GenAI application interfaces. Taking ChatGPT's parent company, OpenAI, as an example, there is a statement on the company website that data input into the application could be used to train future models (OpenAI, 2024). Although it is possible to opt-out of this and choose not to use data to train future models, this is an option that requires pre-existing knowledge and is not turned off by default. However, OpenAI does explicitly state that as models generate a new output each time they are prompted with a question, they are not merely recalling or copying and pasting data that is stored elsewhere. It has been argued though that personal data may be included in GenAI training sets without owner consent. This could result in 'privacy leakage' (Wu et al., 2024). For this reason, the Journal of the American Medical Association (JAMA) group suggests that using GenAI in research should never involve the upload of identifiable information in a dataset (Flanagin et al., 2024). Going further than this, research participants should be informed of how their data, even if anonymised, could be used in a GenAI application at the outset, and an ethical review board should also be made aware of this intention to mitigate ethical issues with data privacy.

Social, Cultural, and Environmental Challenges

Using GenAI in educational research also entails social, cultural, and environmental risk. As GenAI tools are trained on internet data, they mirror the cultural biases and tropes that are present within that data, and for English language GenAI models this entails a Eurocentric view of the world (Roe, 2025). In essence, GenAI is not value free – but rather, for current models at least, contains the biases of the internet, including racism, discrimination, and homophobia (Zhgenti & Holmes, 2023). Use of GenAI in educational research may inadvertently incorporate implicit bias in undetectable or unknown ways, leading to a validity risk for research. On a broader scale, the significance of these biases is that they may lead to the replacement of diverse forms of knowledge and perspectives with a monoculture or a single source of knowledge, thus creating a homogenous body of 'science' (Messeri & Crockett, 2024) or an echo chamber (Turobov et al., 2024). Similarly, Leslie (2023) contends that overreliance or deference to GenAI systems leads to a loss of reflexive practice and given these biases, may reinforce existing hierarchies and socioeconomic divides. This again demonstrates an area where for research purposes, critical pedagogy and its focus on exposing inequities and inequalities has value in exploring GenAI, while the potential for a loss of reflexive practice demands that researchers counteract this with a steadfast focus on reflexivity.

GenAI models may not only contain biases but can also amplify them. A landmark example of this came with text-to-image models such as Stable Diffusion, which was shown to present the world based on a number of concerning stereotypes – including that CEOs are white males, men with dark skin commit crimes, and women with dark skin flip burgers (Nicolleti & Bass, 2023). Further potential sources of bias may not come from the training data, but the developers themselves, as they are involved in fine-tuning output (Alser & Waisberg, 2023). In the worst case, uncritical use of GenAI in educational research could lead to discriminatory science being produced, which damages society (Delios et al., 2024). These biases in training data along the lines of sex, race, age, and worldview may be considered 'hard-coded' into GenAI applications (Peres et al., 2023). Consequently, educational researchers seeking to use GenAI must be sensitive to the possibility of algorithmic bias and consider this actively throughout the research process and consider how such tendencies may affect their own positionality.

A related challenge includes the potential for error if utilising a GenAI model to engage with non-English linguistic data. Wang et al. (2024) examined ChatGPT's ability to understand text in the Paiwan language, noting that the model was unable to distinguish between basic kinship terminology. Partly the reason for this can be attributed to a digital divide – developing countries with less internet access result in less data being produced, which can be employed in training GenAI models (Zhgenti & Holmes, 2023). This could contribute to the marginalization of non-English speakers and the reinforcement of mainstream views (Zhgenti & Holmes, 2023).

A final consideration of whether GenAI use is ethically justified in educational research is the environmental cost of training and using GenAI models. Developing GenAI models has downstream impacts on mining, energy production, and energy consumption which could contribute to the acceleration of climate change (Berthelot et al., 2024). Producing Graphical Processing Units requires rare materials such as cobalt, while other hardware requires multiple forms of natural resources, including plastics (Hosseini et al., 2024). The amount of energy used to create images using image generation models such as Stable Diffusion is large, leading to a shockingly high cost in terms of carbon emissions and potentially contributing to anthropogenic climate change (Heikkilä, 2023; Luccioni et al., 2024). Consequently, the use of GenAI should also be carefully considered given the benefit versus the negative impact on the environment.

Finally, the issue of labour relations and the process by which GenAI models are produced can be evaluated. Training and refinement of these models is often undertaken by employees being paid low wages in the Global South under precarious labour conditions (Williams et al., 2022), while the corporations in the Global North engage in capturing the market. This means that a monopolistic market may develop, thus compounding the unequal labour relations and then limiting the potential for companies in the Global South to participate in the development and benefits of GenAI (Zhgenti & Holmes, 2023). Furthermore, GenAI tools are developed by corporations that may have their own set of socioeconomic interests (Tang, 2024), which may or may not align with the researchers own ethical values. The implications of this for educational researchers are complex, and each individual will need to investigate and come to their own conclusions about the effect that this has when deciding whether to use GenAI for research purposes.

Policy Regulation and Governance

There are multiple calls for national governments and intergovernmental organisations to work together to address GenAI in research, education, training, and data privacy, yet this is still a developing picture. One of the major policy frameworks relevant in this context is the EU AI Act (European Union, 2024), which prohibits certain manipulative or high-risk applications of AI, and ensures that users who are interacting with chatbots or deepfakes must be made aware of the fact they are not interacting with a human. In relation to education, the AI Act points out that AI systems which are used for evaluating learning outcomes, assessments, or monitoring behaviour are classified as high-risk and may violate rights to education if they perpetuate historic biases or discriminate against groups based on age, sexual orientation, gender, racial and ethnic characteristics (European Union, 2024).

It is ultimately these kinds of policy frameworks and legislative directives that will offer apparatuses for accountability and oversight. To this end, the United Nations Educational, Scientific and Cultural Organisation (UNESCO) has also released high-level principles and summaries regarding the use of GenAI in education and research (Miao & Holmes, 2023), which helps to drive key considerations in using GenAI in research, including taking a human-centred approach through proper regulation to ensure transparency. As previously mentioned, this need for transparency applies in multiple uses of GenAI, including analysis of quantitative and qualitative data, writing up results, or assisting with literature reviews. To date however, there are no significant, detailed and specific frameworks or structures on how to assess what is needed to comply with such principles. At the very least, while guidelines are still being developed and implemented, researchers should familiarise themselves with different legal frameworks and jurisdictions and consider these aspects. If a researcher is conducting GenAI-enabled analysis in the European Union, for example, then the requirements of the EU's General Data Protection Act (GDPR) (European Union, 2024) will apply.

From a practical standpoint, education researchers must then commit to remaining up to date and becoming vigilant regarding the evolving legal and policy developments at both national and international levels. While it seems unlikely any policy frameworks will outright ban the use of GenAI tools in research wholesale, the non-compliance with evolving regulations could pose significant challenges – this includes less serious consequences (such as publication rejection) to severe penalties and legal liabilities for violating GDPR. Consequently, adhering to good research practice, such as securing informed consent, anonymising data, verifying GenAI platform compliance with legal frameworks, and disclosing how GenAI tools have been used, can provide the researcher with better assurance that they are conducting integrity-driven ethical research.

The following sections discuss practical use cases for GenAI in educational research. This begins by focusing on the planning and conceptualisation phase of research, followed by literature reviews, quantitative and qualitative data analysis, and the writing up and completion of a manuscript for publication and dissemination. While these are intended to be reference guides and a basis for exploring new technologies in educational research, the above challenges and benefits should be carefully weighed out while engaging with these potential use cases. At the same time, references to published studies and brief summaries of relevant literature are discussed alongside each research stage.

How GenAI Shapes Educational Research Processes

Planning a Research Project

Using GenAI tools to help plan out projects, create ideas, or act as a critical friend through which to discuss and debate the pros and cons of various methods and approaches can be valuable in the early stages of conceiving educational research. The conversational nature of GenAI chatbots like Claude, ChatGPT, and Gemini, makes this an effective use case (Ginde, 2024). While it has been argued that tools like ChatGPT lack the human referential understanding of ideas and concepts (van Manen, 2023), and that they cannot theorise or thematise in the same creative way as humans (van Manen, 2023), this does not negate their benefit in exposing the user to new methodological, theoretical, or practical approaches that exist within the training data of the application, but are unfamiliar to the user. GenAI tools such as ChatGPT can equally provide a broad insight into a topic, give construct definitions and prompt different ways of thinking about existing constructs (Chakravarty, 2024). Although there are no examples of this in educational research literature to date, in the medical field, Nachalon et al. (2024) demonstrated that ChatGPT was able to generate useful research ideas in the area of dysphagia, although its innovative value was limited. For this reason, there is a good argument for using GenAI models to discuss research ideas and plans, and to assist with discussing potential approaches. Multimodal models may be able to generate visualisations of research processes or ideas, including flow charts and diagrams. Caution should be maintained as such models aim to give user-friendly, agreeable advice, to the point of being considered sycophantic (Sharma et al., 2023), thus treating any feedback or ideas suggested with a critical eye should be encouraged.

To demonstrate how this task might be accomplished, an extract is below, using the same prompt with different GenAI models. Note that the outputs have been trimmed to the first subheading of responses for brevity.

Dialogue with GenAI Chatbots: Planning a Project

User: I am preparing for an educational research project, but I'm not sure how to begin tackling my topic. Could you help me consider some ways of planning out the task? My research question is 'How are GenAI tools affecting doctoral researchers in educational studies?'

Response Extract: OpenAI o1-Mini

Certainly! Planning a comprehensive educational research project involves several key steps, from refining your research question to executing your methodology and analyzing your findings. Below is a structured approach tailored to your research question: **'How are GenAI tools affecting doctoral researchers in educational studies?'**

1. **Define the Scope and Objectives**

    a. **Clarify Your Research Question:**

    - Ensure that your research question is specific, measurable, achievable, relevant, and time-bound (SMART).
    - Consider sub-questions, such as:
        - What types of GenAI tools are most commonly used by doctoral researchers in educational studies?
        - How do these tools impact the research process (e.g., data analysis, literature review, writing)?
        - What are the perceived benefits and challenges of using GenAI tools?

Response Extract: DeepSeek-V3

Absolutely! Planning an educational research project can feel overwhelming, but breaking it down into manageable steps will help you stay organized and focused. Below is a structured approach tailored to your research question: *'How are GenAI tools affecting doctoral researchers in educational studies?'*

Step 1: Refine Your Research Question

Your research question is already a great starting point, but you can refine it further by considering:

- **Scope:** Are you focusing on a specific type of GenAI tool (e.g., ChatGPT, Bard, Claude) or all tools broadly?
- **Context**: Are you examining a specific stage of doctoral research (e.g., literature review, data analysis, writing) or the entire research process?

- **Population**: Are you focusing on doctoral researchers in a specific region, institution, or field of educational studies?

    Refined Example:
    How are generative AI tools (e.g., ChatGPT, Bard) impacting the research process, perceptions, and outcomes of doctoral researchers in educational studies in the United States?

    Response Extract: Claude 3.5 – Sonnet
    I'd be happy to help you plan your educational research project. Let's think through some key aspects of investigating AI's impact on doctoral researchers.
    First, let's consider potential research angles:

    1. Looking at how doctoral researchers are using GenAI tools in their work (e.g., literature review, data analysis, and writing).
    2. Examining changes in research practices and methodologies.
    3. Investigating ethical considerations and institutional policies.
    4. Understanding impacts on researcher development and skills acquisition.

In the above examples, ethical use would not involve taking the answers wholesale, copying the resulting text into a file, and submitting it as a research proposal. Rather, these responses provide food for thought and may help the user to better conceptualise what they wish to achieve with their research project. Interestingly, all of the models tested identify that the research question is lacking in specificity and offer actionable solutions to further refine the problem. Two of the outputs give positive feedback (your question is a great starting point!) in an effusive and enthusiastic tone, which may be encouraging but can also be a hallmark of the agreeable and sycophantic tone of GenAI models. For this reason, the user must be aware that this is potentially what they 'want to hear' rather than what they 'need to hear' in planning their project.

Assuming that the user is aware of these tendencies for GenAI models to be sycophantic and agreeable and continues to wish to use a GenAI model for research planning or ideation, users may prompt a chosen model to suggest a list of feasible projects, identify applicable or salient theoretical lenses through which to conduct a study, or ask for detailed feedback. In terms of the challenges of using GenAI in this context, ideas and planning can be considered one of the least problematic. As long as ideation does not involve uploading sensitive personal data or information, and the user is cognizant of the challenges of these models, this can be a helpful way to engage GenAI in the research process. If the user is aiming to create visualisations to help with the planning process (e.g., a Gantt chart) then a multimodal GenAI model may be able to assist in providing an exemplar. Figure 1 illustrates how such a chart may appear:

Example 9-Month Gantt Chart

Task	M1	M2	M3	M4	M5	M6	M7	M8	M9
1. Define Research Scope & Refine Research Questions	■■■	■■■							
2. Literature Review & Theoretical Framework	■■■	■■■	■■■						
3. Ethical Approval (IRB) Process		■■■	■■■						
4. Research Instrument Design & Pilot Testing		■■■	■■■	■■■					
5. Data Collection (Surveys, Interviews, Focus Groups)				■■■	■■■	■■■			
6. Data Cleaning & Analysis					■■■	■■■	■■■		
7. Interpretation & Write-Up of Findings						■■■	■■■	■■■	
8. Revisions & Finalizing Thesis/Paper							■■■	■■■	■■■

Figure 1 An example 9-month Gantt chart produced by OpenAI o1-Mini

Dialogue with a GenAI Chatbot: Creating a Visualisation
User: Can you help me understand how my Gantt chart should look for this research project, assuming I have 9 months to complete it? I need help to visualise what it should look like and what key steps I might have.

OpenAI o1-Mini:
Below is a **sample Gantt Chart** spanning roughly **nine months** for a project investigating the question: **'How are GenAI tools affecting doctoral researchers in educational studies?'**

You can adjust the timelines (e.g., make it shorter or longer) depending on **institutional deadlines, IRB/ethics review timing, participant availability**, and **your personal schedule**. This chart outlines major tasks and their approximate durations.

While the above chart is not perfect, for a single prompt from a user who is unfamiliar with a Gantt chart for planning research, this may be a productive exercise that could help with visualising the planning process. Through repeated prompting, adjustment, and experimentation, the user could eventually produce a visualisation more in line with their research goals and then use that as a template for crafting their own chart. This is one of the use cases where GenAI truly excels.

One significant limitation of using GenAI models in planning educational research relates to the fact that training data is limited and time-bound up to a cut-off date (Ashraf & Ashfaq, 2024). It is possible that new important developments in the field of education, new theoretical approaches, or important similar works will be missed out if the model is prompted to discuss issues like current trends or topics. This may change in future, and it has been argued that soon enough, these models will be connected to academic databases (Rudolph et al., 2023b), which would mitigate this issue, and some GPT-based search tools are connected to the internet. Perplexity.AI is one such case – a search engine which aims to be a 'research partner' by searching the internet and providing up-to-date information with transparent sources (Perplexity, 2024), although Perplexity has also been accused of plagiarising popular media (Shrivastava, 2024). The use of GenAI should be considered as one aspect of the planning process in conjunction with other, human-led efforts to identify gaps in the literature, feasible methodologies, and potential impacts of research, and ultimately human evaluation or 'evaluative judgement' (Bearman et al., 2024) is essential, as in the end it is the responsibility of the researcher who must accept ideas, text, or content which is AI generated (Strzelecki et al., 2024).

The planning phase of research will continue to develop as new models are released. For example, Google's Gemini Deep Research model may act as an agentic AI assistant, drafting a research plan and scouring the internet in order to analyse source material for the user (Google, 2024b). This agentic capability may help researchers to offload ever more of the research process – however the question of validity, hallucinations, and comprehensiveness still remains, and the novelty of these applications and agentic AI may soon come into question as to its practical usefulness. In any case, for educational research projects, the initial planning and idea-generation stage, which can often be one of the most challenging aspects of research for students or those attempting their first scholarly endeavour, can possibly be meaningfully improved through the use of conversational engagement with GenAI agents.

Creating a Literature Review

Embedding research topics into a broader framework within the discipline of study is an essential task, which ensures that research is well formulated, contributes to the current body of knowledge, and rationalises the research question (Zawacki-Richter et al., 2020). This core research activity, that is, the literature review, comes in many forms and varieties, yet requires the researcher at each stage to make decisions about inclusion or exclusion of certain studies through selection criteria, as well as the search strategy, and assessment of study quality (Newman & Gough, 2020). No tools can yet fully automate the literature review process, but AI tools have the potential to contribute to some aspects of this in an educational research context (Haßler et al., 2024). Among the many types of literature review, including but not limited to systematic, scoping, rapid, or narrative, one common feature is shared: reviewing literature takes significant time and labour. Such labour is vital and a core part of the research process itself, generating new insights and developing the researcher's knowledge and understanding of their topic. However, the time-consuming and challenging nature of reviewing literature has led to a focus on whether some, or all, of this task can be offloaded to GenAI tools, again feeding into the narrative that GenAI can assist science by improving the speed and efficiency of research, allowing scholars to do more with less. Consequently, researchers have investigated using ChatGPT to write queries for systematic literature reviews, noting positive results (Ruksakulpiwat et al., 2023).

Using GenAI in a literature review may involve the use of a single discrete task, such as suggesting a search strategy, or may encompass more aspects of the review from generating inclusion and exclusion criteria to assessing the quality of studies against established checklists or benchmarks, or interpreting and synthesising the results of a systematic review. Some of these tasks are more feasible than others. One of the most impractical use cases, to be avoided, is prompting GenAI to produce a list of studies to form the core or basis of a literature review. This task would fail as most current GenAI tools were trained on data only up to a certain cut-off date, which may be several years in the past (although newer models such as OpenAI's Deep Research are now able to access up-to-date documents). However, the most concerning area here is the well-known tendency of GenAI models to fabricate plausible-sounding academic references. Haman & Školník (2024) argue that as ChatGPT cannot be held responsible or liable for its output (the same reason that it cannot be considered an author), it is unethical to use it to assist with literature reviews, and demonstrate this tendency by prompting ChatGPT to produce ten seminal papers in the field of medicine, and noting that in 66 per cent of the results, the references generated simply did not exist. The propensity for hallucinations (Banerjee et al., 2024), fabrication (Emsley, 2023) and sycophantic responses (Sharma et al., 2023) suggests that the core of a literature review cannot be generated by a GenAI model, and similar concerns may apply when prompting a model to assess study quality or interpret findings and results. Even if such an approach were possible, full summarisation and interpretation of literature for a review by a GenAI model may lead to the researcher being unable to develop a deep understanding of each study reviewed.

It is not all bad news. While asking GenAI models to generate a literature review wholesale is not a viable approach, there are different AI tools that have been shown to help doctoral students in producing a quality literature review (Kumar & Gunn, 2024) and may allow users to search for literature in a more targeted manner (Pratschke, 2024). Kumar & Gunn (2024) note that the tools Litmaps, Scholarcy, and Scite may help doctoral students to identify themes, connections, and seminal works in their field, thus streamlining the literature review process and making it seem less of a challenging undertaking. However, the authors recognise that overuse of these tools may risk reliance and that these applications should only be considered a supplement to the literature review process. Other AI-supported tools, such as Rayyan.AI may be helpful for literature screening, while RobotReviewer may assist with quality assessment, and RevMan may help with data analysis and interpretation (Haßler et al., 2024).

A further GenAI tool, Elicit, has received attention for literature review assistance. Elicit searches over 115 million publications from the Semantic Scholar database, and then using semantic similarity measures, identifies related works (Whitfield & Hofmann, 2023), thus producing information and summaries on existing studies. Elicit uses LLM technology to enable researchers to customise the search process, including producing AI-generated summaries and prompting potential research questions. This process can serve as a way of collating relevant documents and fundamentally understanding the field when embarking on an educational research project. That said, Elicit is a new and imperfect tool for literature reviews – findings vary based on the wording of search queries, and certain prompts may be more effective than others. The potential for the researcher to misunderstand the capabilities and applications of Elicit is significant, and the researcher must still evaluate the returned results. Ultimately, Whitfield & Hoffman (2023) posit that Elicit cannot be considered a replacement for literature reviews, but has the potential to reduce some of the burden involved with the process by automating routine tasks. However, in diverse global contexts issues such as the Western-centric algorithmic bias in AI tools, and a lack of available evidence on country and culture-specific educational challenges may impact the viability of GenAI-supported literature reviews in educational research (Haßler et al., 2024).

As with the planning stage, it can be useful for novice researchers who are unfamiliar with literature reviews to use a GenAI model as a conversational agent or personal tutor, as long as they are familiar with the risks and issues outlined at the beginning of this Element. The interaction with a GenAI model below can demonstrate this approach well. The user in this example is seeking to undertake a scoping review for the first time:

> **Dialogue with a GenAI Chatbot: Starting a Scoping Review**
> **User:** As part of my research project, I need to conduct a scoping review on the efficacy of high-stakes language examinations in under-resourced contexts. Which databases should I use? Is there a framework I should follow?
>
> **OpenAI o1-Mini:**
> Below you'll find **key considerations** for planning your scoping review on the efficacy of high-stakes language examinations. The recommendations include **which databases** are most relevant for educational and language-related research, as well as **commonly used frameworks** and guidelines for scoping reviews.
>
> **1. Recommended Databases**
> Given your focus on **high-stakes language examinations** (e.g., IELTS, TOEFL, Cambridge English exams), you'll want databases that cover research in **language education**, **applied linguistics**, **education policy**, and **assessment**. Here are some commonly used databases:
>
> 1. **ERIC (Education Resources Information Centre)**
>   - **Coverage**: Education-specific literature, including language assessment, educational policy, and second-language acquisition research.
>   - **Why Use It**: Often the first port of call for educational research topics.
>
> 2. **LLBA (Linguistics and Language Behaviour Abstracts)**
>   - **Coverage**: Linguistics, language behaviour, applied linguistics, language testing, and assessment.
>   - **Why Use It**: Specializes in language-related research, making it ideal for high-stakes language exam studies.
>
> 3. **Scopus**
>   - **Coverage**: Broad, multidisciplinary database with extensive coverage of peer-reviewed journals, books, and conference proceedings.
>   - **Why Use It**: High citation coverage and advanced search features. Good for cross-disciplinary research.

4. **Web of Science (WoS)**
   - **Coverage**: Multidisciplinary; indexes a wide range of high-impact journals.
   - **Why Use It**: Useful for citation tracking and identifying key authors in the field.

5. **ProQuest Dissertations & Theses**
   - **Coverage**: Theses and dissertations from around the world.
   - **Why Use It**: Can uncover **unpublished studies** and **grey literature**, which is particularly important for scoping reviews aiming for comprehensive coverage.

6. **Education Source (via EBSCOhost)**
   - **Coverage**: Focuses on educational research, pedagogy, policy, and assessment.
   - **Why Use It**: Another robust database with a strong emphasis on international education topics.

7. **Google Scholar** (as a supplemental search)
   - **Coverage**: Broad coverage, including some gray literature, conference papers, and reports.
   - **Why Use It**: Great for snowball searching—checking references in key articles to ensure you're not missing relevant material.

Tip: In addition to these databases, consider searching specialized **assessment and testing journals** (e.g., *Language Testing, Language Assessment Quarterly*) as well as **official test publisher websites** for any technical or validity reports.

User: I would like to follow the PRISMA-ScR framework, how should I approach this?

OpenAI o1-Mini: Below is a concise guide on how to **use the PRISMA extension for Scoping Reviews (PRISMA-ScR)** in your project. This extension, developed by Tricco and colleagues (2018), helps ensure **transparency and rigor** in the planning, conduct, and reporting of a scoping review.

1. **Understand the Purpose of PRISMA-ScR**
   - **PRISMA-ScR** is an **extension** of the original PRISMA (Preferred Reporting Items for Systematic Reviews and Meta-Analyses) statement.

- It **adapts** the systematic review reporting guidelines to **scoping reviews**, which often have broader aims, are more exploratory, and do not always assess the risk of bias or synthesize evidence quantitatively.

Key Reference:

Tricco AC, et al. (2018). *PRISMA extension for scoping reviews (PRISMA-ScR): checklist and explanation.Annals of Internal Medicine*, 169(7), 467–473.

The remainder of the guide from OpenAI's o1-Mini (a paid, subscription-based model) offers sound advice on the procedure for conducting a scoping review following PRISMA-ScR guidelines, but with the potential for the user to enquire, clarify, and repeatedly prompt to find new information or resolve gaps in their knowledge. Note that in this case, the reference provided (Tricco et al., 2018), is correct. Again, using GenAI to assist with developing plans for educational research tasks such as this can be beneficial, as long as it is approached with caution and criticality. In sum, the literature review in educational research is a fundamental and critical activity, yet one that requires a great investment in time and effort. Although GenAI tools may be able to help in terms of a targeted literature search in education specifically (Haßler et al., 2024), they cannot at present be used to generate a literature review themselves. Furthermore, while GenAI tools may be useful 'critical friends' for discussing search strategies, inclusion and exclusion criteria, type of review to undertake, and potential ways of structuring and organising results, this should be seen more as a supportive than an executive function.

Data Analysis

First and foremost, the viability of using GenAI to assist with data analysis requires the researcher to ensure that the chosen analysis methods are valid and are congruent with the philosophical underpinnings of the research project. If a researcher is undertaking a Grounded Theory project with a critical realist ontological position, then there is the potential for an assistive technology such as a GenAI model to identify patterns and meaningful structures that are presumed to independently exist in the research data; thus, there is congruence between the ontology and the use case for GenAI. In this case, efficiency is increased as initial coding may be undertaken more quickly, although the researcher continues to take overall accountability for interpreting the emergent themes. In contrast, a phenomenological approach based on a subjectivist ontology would be unable to assist with interpreting data, as an AI model cannot 'experience' phenomena (i.e., AI lacks *qualia*) and offers a textuality rooted in symbolism, not experience (van Manen, 2023). In this sense, ontology and research design may dictate the use of GenAI.

It has been claimed that GenAI tools could help to 'democratise data analysis' (Inala et al., 2024) through multiple means. This includes eliminating the need for knowledge on generating computer code for executing forms of data analysis, through 'no code' solutions provided by inputting natural language into an LLM or GenAI model, enabling the quick production of code that can assist in data cleaning, transformation, or visualisation of data. Effectively, this removes structural, economic, and knowledge barriers that may hinder some researchers or act as obstacles in their completion of data analysis. At the same time, the familiar issues of hallucination, failure to follow instructions, model biases, and overconfidence in output mitigate these potential benefits (Inala et al. 2024), as do privacy concerns relating to sensitive data. In order to contextualise the possibilities of GenAI at present for data analysis in educational research, the sections are presented primarily along the lines of a quantitative and qualitative distinction, although it is recognised that the reality of analysis may not be such a simple dichotomy.

A Note on Quantitative Data Analysis

There is a comparative lack of research relating to using GenAI for quantitative analysis in comparison to qualitative explorations, and no studies were found in the literature attempting to focus on this aspect in educational research. This may not be a coincidence, given that quantitative research already relies on well-established applications such as SPSS, or the programming languages R and Python. These are time-tested tools that are specifically suited for statistical analysis and thus garner a high degree of trust for reliability and precision. This contrasts with GenAI models such as LLMs which are geared towards natural language processing and do not have the specialised capabilities needed for advanced quantitative analysis. Furthermore, the opaque nature of GenAI outputs and the process by which results are reached may further reduce the attractiveness of using these models in quantitative research. On the other hand, hybrid systems which integrate GenAI into established platforms, for instance by using GenAI capabilities to develop Python scripts for analysis could begin to increase the applicability and popularity of these technologies in quantitative educational research.

One of the ways in which GenAI tools may be used in quantitative educational research is in data cleaning or data entry, although for ethical reasons, and given the privacy challenges described when using tools such as ChatGPT, this should only be done if the data is non-sensitive and publicly available, or it has been approved for sharing with a GenAI model by an ethical review board. Simultaneously, it may be possible to prompt GenAI models to generate code which can automate some of this process, even if the user is not able to complete such coding themselves. GenAI tools which handle multiple forms of input may also be able to assist with data visualisation or interpreting and identifying patterns. This is similar to many other forms of quantitative data analysis tools, but with the added capability of enabling probing and questioning the results and asking for explanations using natural language. There are examples in which quantitative analyses may be possible by uploading data to a GenAI model itself, if it is in line with ethical data handling processes. To demonstrate, Roe & Perkins (2024a) conducted an analysis using ChatGPT of academic integrity policies, which were collected from publicly available institution websites. In this case, as the data is publicly available and likely already used in the training of modern GenAI models, it was deemed ethically appropriate to upload the data files to a platform. If data concerns individuals, is sensitive, or potentially identifying, then this may not be appropriate.

Although there is little published data on the efficiency of using GenAI in complex statistical analysis, Combrinck (2024) contends that using ChatGPT is a perfect environment and highly valid and reliable for producing more basic analyses like descriptive statistics. It is true that to analyse a dataset and produce basic statistical analyses, ChatGPT and other current GenAI models do an impressive job. However, it is still vital to pay close attention to statistical outliers, errors, and issues with interpretation. Running statistical analyses in a GenAI platform could be used for sense-checking, triangulating, or validating existing results, but should not form the main basis of quantitative analytical techniques in a research study. A further application that is relevant for educational research highlighted by (Perkins & Roe, 2024c) is the transformation of quantitative data into visualisations. GenAI tools can generate visual interpretations of data using natural language processing, providing a new lens through which to inspect and understand a dataset. This may then benefit educational researchers by enabling them to gain new insights into data in ways that could have been missed out through traditional analysis. An example of this is the 'artefacts' capability in the newest version of Anthropic's Claude model (Perkins & Roe, 2024c).

Using GenAI models as a learning aid to assist in conducting and teaching about quantitative analysis may also be a suitable approach for novice researchers or those who are still learning a new quantitative method. Combrinck (2024) demonstrates that using ChatGPT as a tutor for statistical methods and quantitative data analysis techniques can support learning. This resonates with one of the popular themes in the literature on Self-Directed

Learning, that GenAI tools can act as an on-demand, personalised teacher (Roe & Perkins, 2024d). In describing the experience of this use case, Combrinck (2024) found that the suggestions are mostly valid. In future, as GenAI models continue to develop, it can be expected that their ability to engage in more complex statistical analyses could improve. At the same time, the open question of hallucination and mistakes will mean that the requirement for human domain expertise and ability to validate and fact-check results may become more, rather than less important.

Qualitative Data Analysis

Qualitative analysis methods are typical in educational research, and common practices include focus groups, interviews, ethnographic and phenomenological approaches. These all result in rich data that can give insight into multiple aspects of educational phenomena. However, qualitative analysis, much like the review and synthesis of literature, requires repeated close readings, rigorous interrogation of the data and a self-reflexive engagement with not only the data, but the positionality of the researcher. Given the propensity for educational research to engage in qualitative analysis, and the in-depth, time-consuming and at times messy realities of such research, it is not surprising that GenAI tools are envisioned as a way to facilitate qualitative research and again, produce efficiencies that ultimately increase speed and automate part of the workload. There is already a growing body of literature exploring how GenAI tools can be used in qualitative analysis, which can be translated to the educational context, and frontier (i.e., the most cutting-edge) models such as ChatGPT, Deepseek, Claude, and Gemini may offer transformative potential by automating data collection, coding, and analyses. For example, GenAI models may be able to enhance the quality of data collection through surveys by assisting with survey design or acting as a 'dummy participant' for a pilot study. GenAI could be used to assist with recruiting participants through creating tailored email recruitment campaigns, or could help to craft data management plans or audit systems and methods for maintaining ethical research practices. At the same time, such uses potentially introduce weak points for maintaining data privacy, and there is a need to make sure that ethical review board applications for research projects point out exactly what third-party applications may be used and how data may be handled. In terms of reflexivity and positionality, the user must also document in consent forms the ways in which GenAI tools may contribute to the research results, and the potential for bias to creep into the analysis.

Qualitative research methods in education often rely on the researcher to be the key instrument (Bogdan & Biklen, 1997), and so it is unlikely that such research could ever be conducted entirely by a nonhuman entity. Yet once qualitative data has been collected and requires further analysis or interpretation, GenAI may be able to offer support. Research has shown that ChatGPT may help to automate the development process of creating codebooks (Barany et al., 2024; van Manen, 2023), and the ability to prompt a model multiple times to shift in focus and pay attention to different aspects of qualitative data may lead the user to deeper insights. A user of a GenAI model for qualitative analysis could be able to use multiple prompts to redirect the model to focus on specific topics of interest, and users can manipulate the number, focus, and type of codes generated (van Manen, 2023).

Other encouraging results using ChatGPT involve qualitative content analysis. Bijker (2024) found through using GenAI in an analysis of forum posts on sugar consumption that, using a dataset of 537 posts, ChatGPT was able to engage in both inductive and deductive analytical processes with a high degree of agreement with human coders. At the same time, the authors suggest that multiple iterations of coding may help with ensuring that the results are reliable. In thematic analysis, GenAI models have been explored for identifying themes in data sets, and research has shown that ChatGPT may be able to process large datasets and distil themes effectively (Yan et al., 2024). Zhang et al. (2024) similarly found that ChatGPT is powerful when coding qualitative data. In the medical context, ChatGPT has been tested for direct coding of transcripts, generating themes from a list of codes, and preprocessing quotes for inclusion in a manuscript (Lee et al., 2024).

Overall, the results of this growing knowledge base suggest that GenAI tools may have an important but supportive place in qualitative educational research. It is unsurprising, therefore, that existing qualitative software packages are beginning to implement GenAI assistance. MaxQDA, NVivo, and ATLAS.ti have already started to include GenAI packages into their products (Wachinger et al., 2024). NVivo specifically, as one of the most prominent examples of a qualitative data analysis tool, now incorporates an AI-assisted autocoding feature to enhance the research process, while MaxQDA offers a tool that enables researchers to 'chat with their data', while maintaining encrypted data protocols and GDPR-compliant data protection (MaxQDA, 2025).

In essence, there are potential uses of GenAI in qualitative analysis in educational research, but with many important caveats. These range from a literate understanding of what the current limitations and capabilities of GenAI technologies are, as well as an understanding of the theoretical and methodological approach which the researcher is taking. Hallucinations, inconsistency, and privacy of sensitive data are all significant obstacles. To elucidate some of these concerns and a potential way through, two brief, fictional scenarios are given next.

Scenario One: An Example of Poor Use of GenAI in Qualitative Educational Research

In this scenario, a researcher receives ethical approval for a study on learner experiences during a new classroom initiative but does not indicate their intention to use a GenAI chatbot to assist with analysis. The researcher uses the chatbot to generate a list of interview questions, but does not vet them first for potential bias, assumptions, or sensitivity. The researcher conducts interviews and transcribes the data. Rather than engage in an in-depth analysis themselves, the researcher uploads the transcripts to the GenAI model and asks for a summary and analysis of the data, and a written section to put into a manuscript. The researcher uses a single prompt, copies the output, and begins working on their manuscript. By doing so, they not only risk sensitive data being compromised, but also do not engage meaningfully with the data they have procured, and meanwhile potentially violate their ethical duties as prescribed by an institutional review board. Furthermore, the researcher has not meaningfully considered one of the key intentions of qualitative research, that is, to capture perspectives accurately (Bogdan & Biklen, 1997), and has violated the academic integrity values of trust and responsibility. While the results may be accepted for publication, at the very core this is a deceptive use of GenAI to increase perceived efficiency while subverting the purpose of qualitative research. As such, this is an example of poor use of GenAI in qualitative educational research.

Scenario Two: An Example of Better Use of GenAI in Qualitative Educational Research

In this scenario, a researcher applies for an ethics exemption to use a publicly available dataset containing qualitative data for an inductive analysis. They are transparent about their intention to engage in an AI-assisted analysis, and have considered the risk/benefit implications and checked their responsibilities under legal and ethical frameworks. The researcher engages with GenAI at the planning stage to share ideas and seek feedback, while maintaining a critical and reflexive set of notes on how they have used the technology. The researcher ultimately crafts their plan and interview questions themselves, relying on GenAI as an assistant. The research participants are fully informed about how GenAI tools will be used for analysing data, and the privacy policy under which their data will be shared. The researcher begins by conducting the analysis themselves using traditional methods, and then attempts to triangulate their results by uploading the dataset to the GenAI model and using multiple, detailed prompts to gain insight into the areas that they may have missed in their analysis, and areas of alignment with the data and their inductive codes. The result of this is that the researcher gains a deeper insight into the data that they are using and potentially uncovers new insights that can embolden their analysis. The researcher transparently declares how the GenAI model was used later in the manuscript. Throughout the process, the researcher reflects on the potential implications for algorithmic bias or errors and considers their own positionality and assumptions about how the use of GenAI may affect their research. This is a better application of GenAI in qualitative educational research.

While the above scenarios represent a very binary set of examples, they are intended to show the way in which GenAI may be used poorly or used more ethically and transparently as a supportive tool. Usage must be transparent, assistive, and carefully considered and planned for – rather than a shortcut to reduce the time required for analysis and get quick results, while undermining the principles that qualitative research is based on. LLMs and other forms of GenAI must be viewed as an adjunct, rather than a replacement, for the qualitative researcher (Kantor, 2024). Given that we are still in the early stages of GenAI development and adoption, it is exciting to see what possibilities will emerge in the coming years for helping to improve research practices, especially in qualitative research in education. At the same time, it is infeasible that qualitative research can be wholly automated by GenAI, given that human agency is an integral part of the process and qualitative analysis requires deep interpretation (Jiang et al., 2021). Furthermore, core aspects of qualitative analysis, such as moments of doubt, serendipity, and discovery, may not be willingly given up by researchers (Jiang et al., 2021).

In the sections on qualitative analysis, most of the focus has been given to the analysis of text collected in the forms of interviews, surveys, and others. However, educational research uses a rich range of methodologies, and it is worth mentioning other GenAI-augmented methods that are only now coming to the fore. One possible example is in ethnographic work, which although derived principally from anthropology, is a common approach in educational research. Seta et al. (2023), for example, explored the use of a new method of 'synthetic ethnography' to investigate the cultural paradigms of GenAI. Boulus-Rødje et al. (2024) employed collaborative autoethnographic methods to understand how academics developed partnerships with GenAI tools in completing work tasks. Each of these examples shows the potential that GenAI can play in differing forms of ethnographic and autoethnographic work. It should not be overlooked that in this section on qualitative data, the focus has been on analysis of transcripts or other forms of textual data. However, educational research is broad and multidisciplinary, and can include many different forms of multimodal data, for example, photographs, videos, sound, or physical artefacts cannot at this time be effectively analysed using GenAI tools. Consequently, this limits the conception of how GenAI can be used in qualitative research, and it should not be assumed that all forms of educational research must revolve around either textual or numeric data.

Reporting and Dissemination of Findings

One of the areas in which GenAI tools have been described as the most effective is in supporting the academic writing process, although this has also generated a considerable amount of controversy. On the one hand, there are critical voices which point out the multiple reasons against using GenAI in tasks such as writing manuscripts or improving the efficiency of research output. Caplan (2024) is one example of the scholarly voices refusing or resisting GenAI use in research and education, on the basis of multiple objections that must be taken seriously, namely that GenAI companies stole copyrighted data for the training of LLMs, that the development of these projects creates significant environmental damage, and the there are many real-world examples of serious harms inflicted by AI technologies, including racist output, election interference, fabricated data, and many more. Noam Chomsky similarly has described ChatGPT as 'high tech plagiarism' (Mohammadzadeh et al., 2023). Other scholars argue that the intensive demands for productivity will result in the academic use of GenAI in tasks like research writing as mandatory, or a fate that academics must accept in order to accelerate 'prestige capture' through publication (Watermeyer et al., 2024). Watermeyer et al. (2024) suggest that this may result in the 'emaciation' of critical or creative skills of academics and result in total dependence on proprietary technologies. Messeri and Crockett (2024) suggest that integrating AI into science is motivated by the imperative to produce more scientific research at greater speeds and at lower cost, thus connecting to the imperative to publish or perish.

Such critiques and resistance to GenAI are important to take seriously, but can be contrasted with more optimistic, yet still suitably cautious perspectives. The literature on using GenAI for scientific writing, publication, and dissemination of results does not advocate for total, uncritical use of these applications, but many do point out numerous possible benefits. Khalifa and Albadawy's (2024) systematic review of twenty-four studies, for example, demonstrates that GenAI usage enhances academic writing in idea generation, content structure, synthesising literature, managing data, editing manuscripts and complying with ethical standards. The authors also point out that using assistive technology in the writing and dissemination of research is not a new phenomenon; reference managers such as Mendeley, EndNote, and Zotero are key examples, as are Digital Writing Assistants such as Grammarly (Roe et al., 2023). Other research has noted that AI-augmented, rather than AI-generated writing can improve how easy manuscripts are to read, enhance linguistic diversity and improve the informativeness of the writing (Hadan et al., 2024).

Just as with data analysis, a fundamental principle is that these models may be best placed as partners, rather than authors (Moya et al., 2023) and researchers must maintain control over the writing process (Hadan et al., 2024). The guidelines suggested by Hadan et al. (2024) for judicious use of GenAI in the writing-up process are adaptable and relevant to educational research. This includes, firstly, openly disclosing how GenAI has been used in the writing process. GenAI disclaimers are now becoming the required norm in scientific writing, required by the Committee on Publication Ethics and media outlets such as Times Higher Education (Moorhouse, 2024), and maintaining this transparency can help to ensure trust in the writing process. Secondly, authors should review, validate, and fact-check any GenAI content. Thirdly, maintaining a 'human touch', as ambiguous as this sounds, can be a vital way of ensuring that research retains the authentic voice of the authors. Although Hadan et al. (2024) do not provide information on what this human touch might be, this could include not copying and pasting GenAI output but using such output to inspire the author's own writing. Such an approach would align well with the fourth recommendation that is to see GenAI as an adjunct, rather than a replacement to the author.

As the use of GenAI in educational research writing evolves, it can be expected that more frameworks and techniques to improve transparency and limit the risk of academic misconduct or errors will come to the fore. Ginde (2024) points out that using processes like checklists, which enable researchers to address issues such as transparency, consistency, and security may help guide the helpful integration of GenAI into research writing. Other similar ideas that have yet to be adopted but show potential in addressing some of these issues include bias assessments. A prominent exemplar is the JAMA network guidance (Flanagin et al., 2024), which recommends reporting a detailed summary of how GenAI models have been used, including the name of the software, version number, manufacturer, dates of use, and description of use, as well as confirmation of taking full responsibility. More detailed checklists and declaration statements may soon be used to help promote transparency in how GenAI is used in the writing and dissemination process. Yan et al. (2024) highlight that another feature that is becoming increasingly common is to pre-register research studies. Pre-registration can be undertaken using public, freely available websites or within an institution's research framework, and during the pre-registration phase, the researcher may be able to document exactly how GenAI will be used throughout the writing up and dissemination process, rather than adding it on only at the time of publication (Yan et al., 2024). This further enhances clarity and transparency in the process. A similar argument is made by Kiley (2024), who advocates for documenting any usage of GenAI in the research process clearly as a way of ensuring transparency.

Other practical uses of GenAI in the writing-up process may be especially suitable for those seeking to publish in English, yet are concerned about their linguistic expression or written proficiency, as mentioned, the additional time required is one of the costs of being an English as Second Language speaker (Amano et al., 2023). In this case, using GenAI chatbots can be extremely helpful, as Huang and Tan (2023) highlight that reviewer criticism of English writing can be tiresome for researchers, who may be advised to seek expertise of a first-language English speaker or even employ a paid service, thus presenting multiple obstacles to publication. This is where GenAI can be beneficial by helping the writer to identify grammatical mistakes, vocabulary issues, and improve the flow and coherence of writing, or provide translations from one language to another. This again may represent a democratising use of the technology in educational research.

Using GenAI tools to help with creative aspects of the writing process may similarly be appropriate. For example, crafting an informative yet also interesting or unique title for a research article can be a challenging task. Biswas (2023) correctly points out that prompting ChatGPT to give multiple iterations of potential titles that effectively capture the meaning and purpose of the research is an acceptable, and positive use of the technology, and that ChatGPT can provide concise and impactful titles encompassing different angles and areas of focus. Ultimately, the research team can then choose that which fits their purpose best, adapting it if necessary and taking responsibility for the final output.

For early career researchers in education, it may be helpful to use GenAI tools like Gemini, ChatGPT, or Claude as a tutor on how to effectively write for specific publications. For novice researchers, scientific writing may be especially difficult and requires a significant time investment (Saccenti et al., 2024). Using a GenAI model not to generate text, but to assist with understanding how to write for a particular outlet or readership, how to follow the guidelines for referencing and citation, and how to format particular aspects of a manuscript could reduce time and effort in preparing a manuscript or selecting an appropriate outlet with the correct target readership. In writing up and disseminating educational research, GenAI tools can also be valuable for tasks such as creating summaries for the public or communicating research outcomes. Many journals currently encourage summaries of research, which can be accessible to a general audience (Misra & Chandwar, 2023). Although the user must be careful to fact-check the accuracy of the output, this is a task which GenAI applications can truly excel at, by summarising in efficient, concise language which can help to communicate findings.

It is also possible to effectively use GenAI to assist with tasks that might not come easily to some educational researchers. For example, obtaining funding through research grants often requires a significant amount of time spent on both identifying opportunities and writing a compelling proposal. GenAI tools specifically developed on helping in the grant writing process such as Grantable.co can be used for identifying and assisting with this key academic task (Kiley, 2024). Seckel et al.'s (2024) rules for using LLMs for grant writing are concise, helpful, and useful for education researchers (despite being written for computational biologists). At the core of these rules is ensuring that the grant funder allows for the use of these technologies and fundamentally, prohibits using AI-generated content for the grant application itself, but encourages use as inspiration for self-generated content. This approach aligns with other literature, which describes how to use GenAI to the researcher's advantage. Lingard (2023) highlights that these tools can intervene when users get 'stuck' in the writing process. A judicious educational researcher can therefore reflect on what aspects of writing up research they find the most challenging, whether it is writing clearly, generating an outline, or deciding a structure, and then consider ways in which GenAI could be used as a critical advisor or collaborator to overcome these challenges. Lingard's (2023) advice to treat anything AI generated as a 'first draft' which is then infused with the writer's own style and voice is an excellent way to view this process.

In summary, while there are critical voices who consider the use of GenAI in scientific writing to be problematic, there is no reason that as a new technology, GenAI cannot be made the best of in appropriate circumstances. Educational research, much like other fields, demands clear communication and linguistic expression in writing, and this is a difficult skill to acquire. In a world where the dominant language of scientific publication is English, this also brings up issues of equality, power, and oppression. Consequently, GenAI can assist with guidance, inspiration, and unblocking those who are struggling to creatively address a topic, as well as removing some of the linguistic obstacles that researchers face. Consequently, using GenAI in research writing is not inherently deceitful (Saccenti et al., 2024), but it must be used wisely and requires dedication from the researcher to becoming AI literate.

Looking to the Future

GenAI has begun to influence a wide range of educational research practices, from rethinking methodological frameworks to raising debates about transparency and academic integrity. As the technology continues to develop, it is set to play an even greater role in reshaping how researchers plan, conduct, and disseminate their work. Although GenAI has already demonstrated its capacity to expedite literature reviews, assist with coding qualitative data, and refine academic writing, researchers are beginning to envision new horizons where GenAI tools become full collaborative partners. This shift is particularly evident in emerging agentic AI models, which aim to delegate more substantial research tasks to intelligent, goal-driven systems, suggesting we may truly be entering a postplagiarism epoch (Eaton, 2023), and long-standing definitions of what it means to be an author may need to radically shift.

In the future, multimodal GenAI platforms could enable researchers to input complex datasets, including text, images, video, and audio, and subsequently generate integrated analyses far more rapidly, changing research processes as we know them. This will lead to further consternation regarding the challenges and obligations of researchers in addressing ethical issues. Questions will persist about how to maintain reflexivity, ensure transparency, and preserve the creative judgment integral to much of educational research, and this can only be addressed through continued dialogue and debate among stakeholders.

Beyond methodological concerns, GenAI could also alter the culture of educational research communities. As these tools become more developed and consistent, it is possible that researchers may start to review traditional research skills as something that can be outsourced. In the education field, it has been found that students may rely on, rather than learn from GenAI in certain tasks (Darvishi et al., 2024), and the same could in theory apply to researchers. While such outsourcing may be helpful, this overreliance could risk eroding important skills, such as deep creating and critical thinking. Consequently, universities and research institutions may need to develop a set of guidelines that describe how these tools can be used in educational research without undermining such foundational skills.

The global dimension of GenAI in educational research should also not be overlooked. Researchers in different linguistic and cultural contexts may find that GenAI models offer better access to scientific literature or are helpful in publishing in an English-dominated scholarly landscape, and this could lead to a great range of perspectives and more representation of studies from underrepresented global contexts. On the other hand, political and economic conflicts at the international level may result in the benefits of GenAI being reaped only by those with the funds and abilities to access these technologies, potentially growing the digital divide and negatively impacting inclusivity in the field of education.

Conclusion

This Element has sought to provide an initial guide to the considerations of using GenAI in educational research, with practical guidance on potential ways to use GenAI for benefit. Finding a way through the maze of information on GenAI is complex. These technologies are dynamic, quickly evolving, and being developed in increasingly volatile, politically and economically charged environments. The big questions surrounding frontier models are now switching towards issues of censorship, ownership, and access, and the coming years will see many more disruptions as GenAI continues to become integrated with day-to-day lives around the world.

For educational researchers, there are potential benefits to be reaped from the use of GenAI at every stage of the research process. From initial ideation through to dissemination of completed research, it is possible to use AI and GenAI technologies effectively, ethically, and responsibly. GenAI models should not be anthropomorphised, and it is important not to mistake the interchanges that we have them for real, human interactions. The nature of responses is a product of training data, not thought and lived experience, and the knowledge produced may be accurate, but is routinely incorrect. A high level of criticality, scepticism, and questioning can help to reduce some of the risks associated with using GenAI in educational research, but the onus is on both the research community and the individual to seek out information, critically analyse the potential for ethical impacts, and share information on best practice. Finally, by analysing and understanding what GenAI cannot do, we are able to gain a better appreciation of the incredible attributes that humans bring to the table as skilled practitioners and curious researchers, capable of producing new scientific knowledge and contributing to an understanding how humans learn and develop. Although time will tell whether GenAI ever approximates human intelligence and skills, it can be assured that the role and importance of the researcher are becoming more central to educational research, rather than less so.

How GenAI Was Used in This Element

Generative AI tools were used in developing this manuscript in a variety of ways. As a researcher in GenAI and education, I have been using these technologies on a near-daily basis since 2022. I document and record my reflections throughout the research and writing process to maintain reflexivity. However, I am aware that because of my use of these technologies, I may make assumptions when communicating with the reader. I relied on formal and informal peer review feedback on the draft manuscript to help alleviate this challenge.

Experimentation with a variety of GenAI models was important for developing and creating the content of the Element, including the uses, benefits, and risks of these technologies for different educational research tasks. I used GenAI models to attempt various tasks, for example, generating reference lists, checking and verifying data interpretations, or developing passages of dummy text. I used several models to generate example outputs to illustrate points, as can be seen in the section 'How GenAI Shapes Educational Research Processes'. The models used in this capacity are:

Claude 3.5 Sonnet (Anthropic)
Deepseek V3
OpenAI o1-Mini

Aside from these exemplars, I did not use GenAI models to generate text directly for the Element, but I did upload excerpts of drafts for 'critical feedback' and suggestions for rewrites, phrasing and edits. I relied on OpenAI's GPT4.5 Research Preview and o4-mini-high for these suggestions. These models at the time of writing required a paid, premium subscription service. I chose these models because of familiarity and personal preference.

Finally, OpenAI's o4-mini-high was used to help draft and generate a checklist for GenAI use in Educational Research. Drawing on the content of the work I have presented here, I developed a list of key topics for the checklist and prompted the model to organise them into a sequential list. The initial output was then used as a basis for revision and editing, before being developed with peer (human) feedback and critical reflection to arrive at the final checklist, which is below. As the author, I take full responsibility for the accuracy, veracity, and ownership of this work.

A Checklist for GenAI Use in Educational Research

The below is a non-exhaustive checklist which can be used to identify key considerations in using GenAI for educational research tasks, organised into eight subheadings.

1. **Ethical Approval, Academic and Research Integrity**

    - Secure ethical approval before using any GenAI model in your research and be clear in your applications to ethical review boards on how and why you intend to use GenAI.
    - Make sure that informed consent includes GenAI processing of participant data if applicable, and explain any risks involved.

- Never present AI-generated content as human-authored and always ensure you explain how GenAI has been used.
- Check guidelines and policies from funding organisations and publishers before using any GenAI model.

2. **Transparency and Documenting Use**

   - Create a file or folder with details on how you have used GenAI.
   - Document prompts, models and versions used, along with the date.
   - Keep a changelog of AI-assisted drafts, edits, and analysis.
   - Report your workflow and process of using GenAI so others can understand how it was used.

3. **Data Privacy & Security**

   - Make sure no identifying details or sensitive data is uploaded into third-party GenAI models.
   - Check the platform's data retention and training-use policies before using it.
   - Ensure you are complying with relevant privacy and data regulations (e.g., GDPR).

4. **Bias Mitigation**

   - Reflect on outputs and seek to identify any potential demographic, cultural, or ideological biases.
   - Use multiple models or additional human review to triangulate findings and identify any blind spots or errors.

5. **Quality and Accuracy**

   - Fact-check any AI-generated claims using primary source material. Ensure any statistical or interpretive outputs are verified and checked by humans with subject expertise.
   - Never accept AI-generated material as factually correct without external verification. Although newer 'deep research' models may be able to identify source material within the output window.

6. **Replicability and Reliability**

   - Consider documenting your prompts and responses for reporting or archiving if practicable.
   - Run key prompts several times to identify variability in outputs.
   - Acknowledge the black-box nature of GenAI within your research's limitations section.

7. **Positionality and Reflexivity**
   - Engage in reflexivity when using GenAI, and consider using reflexive journalling to document why and how you used the technology.
   - Consider using peer debriefing or peer review to help critique your use of GenAI.

8. **Staying up to date**
   - Seek up-to-date resources on new models and risk considerations.
   - Ensure you are aware of any significant changes to relevant legislation (e.g., the EU AI Act).
   - Explore emerging methods of minimising ethical issues (e.g., open source models).
   - Disclose your compliance strategies, GenAI use, and process in funding applications, publications, and proposals.

References

Academ-AI. (2024). *Suspected AI*. www.academ-ai.info/.

Adams, P. (2006). Exploring social constructivism: Theories and practicalities. *Education*. https://doi.org/10.1080/03004270600898893

Alm, A., & Watanabe, Y. (2023). Integrating ChatGPT in language education: A freirean perspective. *Iranian Journal of Language Teaching Research, 11*(3 (Special Issue)), 19–30. https://doi.org/10.30466/ijltr.2023.121404.

Alser, M., & Waisberg, E. (2023). Concerns with the usage of ChatGPT in academia and medicine: A viewpoint. *American Journal of Medicine Open, 9*, 100036. https://doi.org/10.1016/j.ajmo.2023.100036.

Al-Zahrani, A. M. (2024). The impact of generative AI tools on researchers and research: Implications for academia in higher education. *Innovations in Education and Teaching International, 61*(5), 1029–1043. https://doi.org/10.1080/14703297.2023.2271445.

Amano, T., Ramírez-Castañeda, V., Berdejo-Espinola, V., et al. (2023). The manifold costs of being a non-native English speaker in science. *PLOS Biology, 21*(7), e3002184. https://doi.org/10.1371/journal.pbio.3002184.

Ansari, A. N., Ahmad, S., & Bhutta, S. M. (2024). Mapping the global evidence around the use of ChatGPT in higher education: A systematic scoping review. *Education and Information Technologies, 29*(9), 11281–11321. https://doi.org/10.1007/s10639-023-12223-4.

Ariyaratne, S., Iyengar, K. P., & Botchu, R. (2023). Will collaborative publishing with ChatGPT drive academic writing in the future? *British Journal of Surgery, 110*(9), 1213–1214. https://doi.org/10.1093/bjs/znad198.

Arkoudas, K. (2023). ChatGPT is no stochastic parrot. but it also claims that 1 is greater than 1. *Philosophy & Technology, 36*(3), 1–29. https://doi.org/10.1007/s13347-023-00619-6.

Ashraf, H., & Ashfaq, H. (2024). The role of ChatGPT in medical research: Progress and limitations. *Annals of Biomedical Engineering, 52*(3), 458–461. https://doi.org/10.1007/s10439-023-03311-0.

Asmawi, A., & Alam, Md. S. (2024). Understanding the digital epistemologies of Chat GPT: Towards a decolonial language pedagogy. *Proceedings of the 2024 8th International Conference on Digital Technology in Education (ICDTE)*, 277–283. https://doi.org/10.1145/3696230.3696248.

Banerjee, S., Agarwal, A., & Singla, S. (2024). *LLMs Will Always Hallucinate, and We Need to Live With This* (No. arXiv:2409.05746). arXiv. https://doi.org/10.48550/arXiv.2409.05746.

References

Banh, L., & Strobel, G. (2023). Generative artificial intelligence. *Electronic Markets*, *33*(1), 1–17. https://doi.org/10.1007/s12525-023-00680-1.

Barany, A., Nasiar, N., Porter, C., et al. (2024). ChatGPT for education research: Exploring the potential of large language models for qualitative codebook development. In A. M. Olney, I.-A. Chounta, Z. Liu, O. C. Santos, & I. I. Bittencourt (Eds.), *Artificial Intelligence in Education* (pp. 134–149). Springer Nature Switzerland. https://doi.org/10.1007/978-3-031-64299-9_10.

Barros, A., Prasad, A., & Śliwa, M. (2023). Generative artificial intelligence and academia: Implication for research, teaching and service. *Management Learning*, *54*(5), 597–604. https://doi.org/10.1177/13505076231201445.

Basit, T. N. (2013). Ethics, reflexivity and access in educational research: Issues in intergenerational investigation. *Research Papers in Education*, *28*(4), 506–517. https://doi.org/10.1080/02671522.2012.689318.

Baskara, F. R. (2024). ChatGPT and critical digital pedagogy: Examining the potential and challenges for educational practice. *Proceeding of the International Conference of Inovation, Science, Technology, Education, Children, and Health*, *4*(1), Article 1.

Bearman, M., & Ajjawi, R. (2023). Learning to work with the black box: Pedagogy for a world with artificial intelligence. *British Journal of Educational Technology*, *54*(5), 1160–1173. https://doi.org/10.1111/bjet.13337.

Bearman, M., Tai, J., Dawson, P., Boud, D., & Ajjawi, R. (2024). Developing evaluative judgement for a time of generative artificial intelligence. *Assessment & Evaluation in Higher Education*, *49*(6), 893–905. https://doi.org/10.1080/02602938.2024.2335321.

Bender, E. M., Gebru, T., McMillan-Major, A., & Shmitchell, S. (2021). On the dangers of stochastic parrots: Can language models be too big? *Proceedings of the 2021 ACM Conference on Fairness, Accountability, and Transparency*, 610–623. https://doi.org/10.1145/3442188.3445922.

Berthelot, A., Caron, E., Jay, M., & Lefèvre, L. (2024). Estimating the environmental impact of Generative-AI services using an LCA-based methodology. *Procedia CIRP*, *122*, 707–712. https://doi.org/10.1016/j.procir.2024.01.098.

Bijker, R., Merkouris, S. S., Dowling, N. A., & Rodda, S. N. (2024). ChatGPT for automated qualitative research: Content analysis. *Journal of Medical Internet Research*, *26*(1), e59050. https://doi.org/10.2196/59050.

Bin-Nashwan, S. A., Sadallah, M., & Bouteraa, M. (2023). Use of ChatGPT in academia: Academic integrity hangs in the balance. *Technology in Society*, *75*, 102370. https://doi.org/10.1016/j.techsoc.2023.102370.

Bishop, J. M. (2021). Artificial intelligence is stupid and causal reasoning will not fix it. *Frontiers in Psychology*, *11*, 1–18. https://doi.org/10.3389/fpsyg.2020.513474.

Biswas, S. S. (2023). ChatGPT for research and publication: A step-by-step guide. *The Journal of Pediatric Pharmacology and Therapeutics*, *28*(6), 576–584. https://doi.org/10.5863/1551-6776-28.6.576.

Bjelobaba, S., Waddington, L., Perkins, M., et al. (2024). *Research Integrity and GenAI: A Systematic Analysis of Ethical Challenges across Research Phases* (No. arXiv:2412.10134). arXiv. https://doi.org/10.48550/arXiv.2412.10134.

Bogdan, R., & Biklen, S. K. (1997). *Qualitative Research for Education* (Vol. 368). Allyn & Bacon Boston, MA. http://math.buffalostate.edu/dwilson/med595/qualitative_intro.pdf.

Boulus-Rødje, N., Cranefield, J., Doyle, C., & Fleron, B. (2024). GenAI and me: The hidden work of building and maintaining an augmentative partnership. *Personal and Ubiquitous Computing*. https://doi.org/10.1007/s00779-024-01810-y.

Bozkurt, A. (2023). Generative artificial intelligence (AI) powered conversational educational agents: The inevitable paradigm shift. *Asian Journal of Distance Education*, *18*(1), 198–204. https://doi.org/10.5281/zenodo.7716416.

Bridgeman, A., Liu, D., & Weeks, R. (2024). *Program level assessment design and the two-lane approach – Teaching@Sydney*. https://educational-innovation.sydney.edu.au/teaching@sydney/program-level-assessment-two-lane/.

Bringula, R. (2025). What do academics have to say about ChatGPT? A text mining analytics on the discussions regarding ChatGPT on research writing. *AI and Ethics*, *5*, 371–383. https://doi.org/10.1007/s43681-023-00354-w.

Burger, B., Kanbach, D. K., Kraus, S., Breier, M., & Corvello, V. (2023). On the use of AI-based tools like ChatGPT to support management research. *European Journal of Innovation Management*, *26*(7), 233–241. https://doi.org/10.1108/EJIM-02-2023-0156.

Caplan, N. (2024). *Is It a Chatbot or a False Dichotomy*. Nigel Caplan. https://nigelcaplan.com/.

Chadwick, L. (2024). *Could Microsoft's new AI feature really correct hallucinations?* Euronews. www.euronews.com/next/2024/09/26/microsoft-claims-its-new-ai-correction-feature-can-fix-hallucinations-does-it-work.

Chakravarty, A. (2024). Research note 'replicating published literature review using ChatGPT-plus: Observations'. *Customer Needs and Solutions*, *11*(1), 1–6. https://doi.org/10.1007/s40547-024-00144-3.

Chan, C. K. Y., & Colloton, T. (2024). *Generative AI in Higher Education: The ChatGPT Effect*. Taylor & Francis Group. http://ebookcentral.proquest.com/lib/jcu/detail.action?docID=31281986.

Cobern, W. W. (1993). Constructivism. *Journal of Educational and Psychological Consultation*, *4*(1), 105–112. https://doi.org/10.1207/s1532768xjepc0401_8.

Coghlan, D., & Brydon-Miller, M. (2014). Positionality. In Coghlan, D., & Brydon-Miller, M. (Eds.), *The SAGE Encyclopedia of Action Research* (pp. 628–628). SAGE. https://doi.org/10.4135/9781446294406.

Combrinck, C. (2024). A tutorial for integrating generative AI in mixed methods data analysis. *Discover Education*, *3*(1), 1–23. https://doi.org/10.1007/s44217-024-00214-7.

Cotton, D. R. E., Cotton, P. A., & Shipway, J. R. (2024). Chatting and cheating: Ensuring academic integrity in the era of ChatGPT. *Innovations in Education and Teaching International*, *61*(2), 228–239. https://doi.org/10.1080/14703297.2023.2190148.

Dalalah, D., & Dalalah, O. M. A. (2023). The false positives and false negatives of generative AI detection tools in education and academic research: The case of ChatGPT. *The International Journal of Management Education*, *21*(2), 100822. https://doi.org/10.1016/j.ijme.2023.100822.

Daniel, S. J. (2020). Education and the COVID-19 pandemic. *PROSPECTS*, *49*(1), 91–96. https://doi.org/10.1007/s11125-020-09464-3.

Darder, A., Hernandez, K., Lam, K. D., & Baltodano, M. (2023). Critical pedagogy: An introduction. In *The critical pedagogy reader* (pp. 1–30). Routledge.

Darvishi, A., Khosravi, H., Sadiq, S., Gašević, D., & Siemens, G. (2024). Impact of AI assistance on student agency. *Computers & Education*, *210*, 104967. https://doi.org/10.1016/j.compedu.2023.104967.

Day, T. (2023). A preliminary investigation of fake peer-reviewed citations and references generated by ChatGPT. *The Professional Geographer*, *75*(6), 1024–1027. https://doi.org/10.1080/00330124.2023.2190373.

Delios, A., Tung, R. L., & van Witteloostuijn, A. (2025). How to intelligently embrace generative AI: The first guardrails for the use of GenAI in IB research. *Journal of International Business Studies*. *56*, 451–460. https://doi.org/10.1057/s41267-024-00736-0.

Deng, R., Jiang, M., Yu, X., Lu, Y., & Liu, S. (2025). Does ChatGPT enhance student learning? A systematic review and meta-analysis of experimental studies. *Computers & Education*, *227*, 105224. https://doi.org/10.1016/j.compedu.2024.105224.

Devlin, J., Chang, M.-W., Lee, K., & Toutanova, K. (2019). *BERT: Pre-training of Deep Bidirectional Transformers for Language Understanding* (No. arXiv:1810.04805). arXiv. https://doi.org/10.48550/arXiv.1810.04805.

Dowling, M., & Lucey, B. (2023). ChatGPT for (Finance) research: The Bananarama Conjecture. *Finance Research Letters, 53*, 103662. https://doi.org/10.1016/j.frl.2023.103662.

Downes, S. (2022). Connectivism. *Asian Journal of Distance Education, 17*(1), Article 1. https://asianjde.com/ojs/index.php/AsianJDE/article/view/623.

Eaton, S. E. (2022). The academic integrity technological arms race and its impact on learning, teaching, and assessment. *Canadian Journal of Learning and Technology, 48*(2), Article 2. https://doi.org/10.21432/cjlt28388.

Eaton, S. E. (2023). Postplagiarism: Transdisciplinary ethics and integrity in the age of artificial intelligence and neurotechnology. *International Journal for Educational Integrity, 19*(1), Article 1. https://doi.org/10.1007/s40979-023-00144-1.

Emsley, R. (2023). ChatGPT: These are not hallucinations – they're fabrications and falsifications. *Schizophrenia, 9*(1), 1–2. https://doi.org/10.1038/s41537-023-00379-4.

European Union. (n.d.). *The General Data Protection Regulation*. Consilium. Retrieved December 21, 2024, www.consilium.europa.eu/en/policies/data-protection/data-protection-regulation/.

European Union. (2024). *High-Level Summary of the AI Act | EU Artificial Intelligence Act*. https://artificialintelligenceact.eu/high-level-summary/.

Flanagin, A., Pirracchio, R., Khera, R., et al. (2024). Reporting use of AI in research and scholarly publication—JAMA network guidance. *JAMA, 331*(13), 1096–1098. https://doi.org/10.1001/jama.2024.3471.

Floridi, L. (2020). AI and its new winter: From myths to realities. *Philosophy & Technology, 33*(1), 1–3. https://doi.org/10.1007/s13347-020-00396-6.

Floridi, L. (2024). Why the AI hype is another tech bubble. *Philosophy & Technology, 37*(4), 1–13. https://doi.org/10.1007/s13347-024-00817-w.

Freire, P. (2000). *Pedagogy of the Oppressed* (30th anniversary ed). Continuum.

Furze, L., Perkins, M., Roe, J., & MacVaugh, J. (2024). The AI assessment scale (AIAS) in action: A pilot implementation of GenAI-supported assessment. *Australasian Journal of Educational Technology, 40*(4), Article 4. https://doi.org/10.14742/ajet.9434.

Gamage, K. A. A., Silva, E. K. de, & Gunawardhana, N. (2020). Online delivery and assessment during COVID-19: Safeguarding academic integrity. *Education Sciences, 10*(11), Article 11. https://doi.org/10.3390/educsci10110301.

Gaumann, Noëlle & Veale, Michael (2024). AI providers as criminal essay mills? Large language models meet contract cheating law. *Information and Communications Technology Law* 10.1080/13600834.2024.2352692. (In press).

George, A. S. (2023). The potential of generative AI to reform graduate education. *Partners Universal International Research Journal*, *2*(4), 36–50.

Gilson, A., Safranek, C. W., Huang, T., et al. (2023). How does ChatGPT perform on the United States Medical Licensing Examination (USMLE)? The implications of large language models for medical education and knowledge assessment. *JMIR Medical Education*, *9*, e45312. https://doi.org/10.2196/45312.

Ginde, G. (2024). *'So What If I Used GenAI?' – Implications of Using Cloud-Based GenAI in Software Engineering Research* (No. arXiv:2412.07221). arXiv. https://doi.org/10.48550/arXiv.2412.07221.

Goldman Sachs. (2024). *AI Investment Forecast to Approach $200 Billion Globally by 2025*. www.goldmansachs.com/insights/articles/ai-investment-forecast-to-approach-200-billion-globally-by-2025.

Google. (2024a). *Google NotebookLM | Note Taking & Research Assistant Powered by AI*. https://notebooklm.google/.

Google. (2024b). *Try Deep Research and our New Experimental Model in Gemini, your AI Assistant*. https://blog.google/products/gemini/google-gemini-deep-research/.

Goto, A., & Katanoda, K. (2023). Should we acknowledge ChatGPT as an author? *Journal of Epidemiology*, *33*(7), 333–334. https://doi.org/10.2188/jea.JE20230078.

GOV. (2025). *Generative Artificial Intelligence (AI) in Education*. GOV.UK. www.gov.uk/government/publications/generative-artificial-intelligence-in-education/generative-artificial-intelligence-ai-in-education.

Gray, A. (2024). *ChatGPT 'Contamination': Estimating the Prevalence of LLMs in the Scholarly Literature* (No. arXiv:2403.16887). arXiv. https://doi.org/10.48550/arXiv.2403.16887.

Grubaugh, S., Levitt, G., & Deever, D. (2023). Harnessing AI to power constructivist learning: An evolution in educational methodologies. *EIKI Journal of Effective Teaching Methods*, *1*(3), Article 3. https://doi.org/10.59652/jetm.v1i3.43.

Grzybowski, A., Pawlikowska–Łagód, K., & Lambert, W. C. (2024). A history of artificial intelligence. *Clinics in Dermatology*, *42*(3), 221–229. https://doi.org/10.1016/j.clindermatol.2023.12.016.

Hadan, H., Wang, D. M., Mogavi, R. H., et al. (2024). The great AI witch hunt: Reviewers' perception and (Mis)conception of generative AI in research writing. *Computers in Human Behavior: Artificial Humans, 2*(2), 100095. https://doi.org/10.1016/j.chbah.2024.100095.

Haman, M., & Školník, M. (2024). Using ChatGPT to conduct a literature review. *Accountability in Research, 31*(8), 1244–1246. https://doi.org/10.1080/08989621.2023.2185514.

Han, J., Qiu, W., & Lichtfouse, E. (2024). ChatGPT in scientific research and writing: A beginner's guide. In J. Han, W. Qiu, & E. Lichtfouse (Eds.), *ChatGPT in Scientific Research and Writing: A Beginner's Guide* (pp. 1–109). Springer Nature Switzerland. https://doi.org/10.1007/978-3-031-66940-8_1.

Haßler, B., Hassan, S. M., Klune, C., Mansour, H., & Friese, L. (2024). *Using AI to Automate the Literature Review Process in Education: A Topic Brief* (No. 183). EdTech Hub. https://doi.org/10.53832/edtechhub.1003.

Heikkilä, M. (2023). *Making an Image with Generative AI Uses as Much Energy as Charging Your Phone | MIT Technology Review*. www.technologyreview.com/2023/12/01/1084189/making-an-image-with-generative-ai-uses-as-much-energy-as-charging-your-phone/.

Herweijer, C. (2018, January 24). *8 Ways AI Can Help Save the Planet*. World Economic Forum. www.weforum.org/stories/2018/01/8-ways-ai-can-help-save-the-planet/.

Hicks, M. T., Humphries, J., & Slater, J. (2024). ChatGPT Is Bullshit. *Ethics and Information Technology, 26*(2), 1–10. https://doi.org/10.1007/s10676-024-09775-5.

Honig, C. (2024). GenAI Teachers: Constructivist Learning Design and Value Propositions. *ASCILITE Publications*, 287–297. https://doi.org/10.14742/apubs.2024.1487.

Hoskins, P., & Rahman-Jones. (2025, January 27). *DeepSeek: Chinese AI Model Rockets to Top of App Charts*. BBC News. www.bbc.com/news/articles/c0qw7z2v1pgo.

Hosseini, M., Gao, P., & Vivas-Valencia, C. (2024). A social-environmental impact perspective of generative artificial intelligence. *Environmental Science and Ecotechnology*, 100520. https://doi.org/10.1016/j.ese.2024.100520.

Hosseini, M., & Horbach, S. P. J. M. (2023). Fighting reviewer fatigue or amplifying bias? Considerations and recommendations for use of ChatGPT and other large language models in scholarly peer review. *Research Integrity and Peer Review, 8*(1), 1–9. https://doi.org/10.1186/s41073-023-00133-5.

Huang, L., Yu, W., Ma, W., et al. (2024). A survey on hallucination in large language models: Principles, taxonomy, challenges, and open questions. *ACM Transactions on Information Systems*, 3703155. https://doi.org/10.1145/3703155.

Hurley, Z. (2024). Generative AI's family portraits of whiteness: A postdigital semiotic case study. *Postdigital Science and Education*, *6*(4), 1240–1260. https://doi.org/10.1007/s42438-024-00491-3.

IBM. (2024). *What Is Generative AI?* www.ibm.com/think/topics/generative-ai.

Inala, J. P., Wang, C., Drucker, S., et al. (2024). *Data Analysis in the Era of Generative AI* (No. arXiv:2409.18475). arXiv. https://doi.org/10.48550/arXiv.2409.18475.

Jiang, J. A., Wade, K., Fiesler, C., & Brubaker, J. R. (2021). Supporting serendipity: Opportunities and challenges for human-AI collaboration in qualitative analysis. *Proceedings of the ACM on Human-Computer Interaction*, *5*(CSCW1), 1–23. https://doi.org/10.1145/3449168.

Jin, Y., Yan, L., Echeverria, V., Gašević, D., & Martinez-Maldonado, R. (2025). Generative AI in higher education: A global perspective of institutional adoption policies and guidelines. *Computers and Education: Artificial Intelligence*, *8*, 100348. https://doi.org/10.1016/j.caeai.2024.100348.

Kantor, J. (2024). Best practices for implementing ChatGPT, large language models, and artificial intelligence in qualitative and survey-based research. *JAAD International*, *14*, 22–23. https://doi.org/10.1016/j.jdin.2023.10.001.

Kaplan, A., & Haenlein, M. (2019). Siri, Siri, in my hand: Who's the fairest in the land? On the interpretations, illustrations, and implications of artificial intelligence. *Business Horizons*, *62*(1), 15–25. https://doi.org/10.1016/j.bushor.2018.08.004.

Khalifa, M., & Albadawy, M. (2024). Using artificial intelligence in academic writing and research: An essential productivity tool. *Computer Methods and Programs in Biomedicine Update*, *5*, 100145. https://doi.org/10.1016/j.cmpbup.2024.100145.

Kiley, J. (2024). *Chapter 6: Benefits, Pitfalls, Ethics and Realities of GenAI in Research*. www.elgaronline.com/edcollchap/book/9781035332724/book-part-9781035332724-12.xml.

Kousha, K. (2024). How is ChatGPT acknowledged in academic publications? *Scientometrics*, *129*(12), 7959–7969. https://doi.org/10.1007/s11192-024-05193-y.

Kumar, S., & Gunn, A. (2024). Doctoral students' reflections on generative artificial intelligence (GenAI) use in the literature review process. *Innovations in Education and Teaching International*, *62*(4), 1395–1408. https://doi.org/10.1080/14703297.2024.2427049.

Lee, V. V., Lubbe, S. C. C. van der, Goh, L. H., & Valderas, J. M. (2024). Harnessing ChatGPT for thematic analysis: Are we ready? *Journal of Medical Internet Research*, *26*(1), e54974. https://doi.org/10.2196/54974.

Leslie, D. (2023). Does the sun rise for ChatGPT? Scientific discovery in the age of generative AI. *AI and Ethics*. https://doi.org/10.1007/s43681-023-00315-3.

Liang, E. S., & Bai, S. (2024). Generative AI and the future of connectivist learning in higher education. *Journal of Asian Public Policy*, *18*(1), 1–23. https://doi.org/10.1080/17516234.2024.2386085.

Liang, W., Yuksekgonul, M., Mao, Y., Wu, E., & Zou, J. (2023). *GPT Detectors are Biased against Non-native English Writers* (No. arXiv:2304.02819). arXiv. https://doi.org/10.48550/arXiv.2304.02819.

Limo, F. A. F., Tiza, D. R. H., Roque, M. M., et al. (2023). Personalized tutoring: ChatGPT as a virtual tutor for personalized learning experiences. *Przestrzeń Społeczna (Social Space)*, *23*(1), Article 1.

Lingard, L. (2023). Writing with ChatGPT: An illustration of its capacity, limitations & implications for academic writers. *Perspectives on Medical Education*, *12*(1), 261–270. https://doi.org/10.5334/pme.1072.

Liu, C. H., & Matthews, R. (2005). Vygotsky's Philosophy: Constructivism and Its Criticisms Examined. *International Education Journal*, *6*(3), 386–399.

Luccioni, A. S., Jernite, Y., & Strubell, E. (2024). Power hungry processing: Watts driving the cost of AI deployment? *The 2024 ACM Conference on Fairness, Accountability, and Transparency*, 85–99. https://doi.org/10.1145/3630106.3658542.

Macfarlane, B., Zhang, J., & Pun, A. (2014). Academic integrity: A review of the literature. *Studies in Higher Education*, *39*(2), 339–358. https://doi.org/10.1080/03075079.2012.709495.

MaxQDA. (2025). *AI Data Protection*. www.maxqda.com/ai-data-protection.

McMahon, L., Kleinman, Z., & Edwards. (2025, January 12). *Artificial Intelligence: Plan to 'Unleash AI' across UK Revealed*. BBC News. www.bbc.com/news/articles/crr05jykzkxo.

Messeri, L., & Crockett, M. J. (2024). Artificial intelligence and illusions of understanding in scientific research. *Nature*, *627*(8002), 49–58. https://doi.org/10.1038/s41586-024-07146-0.

Miao, F., & Holmes, W. (2023). *Guidance for Generative AI in Education and Research | UNESCO*. www.unesco.org/en/articles/guidance-generative-ai-education-and-research.

Misra, D. P., & Chandwar, K. (2023). ChatGPT, artificial intelligence and scientific writing: What authors, peer reviewers and editors should know. *Journal of the Royal College of Physicians of Edinburgh*, *53*(2), 90–93. https://doi.org/10.1177/14782715231181023.

Mohammadzadeh, Z., Ausloos, M., & Saeidnia, H. R. (2023). ChatGPT: High-tech plagiarism awaits academic publishing green light. Non-fungible token (NFT) can be a way out. *Library Hi Tech News, 40*(7), 12–14. https://doi.org/10.1108/LHTN-04-2023-0067.

Moorhouse, B. L. (2024). *We're Living in a World of Artificial Intelligence – It's Academic Publishing that Needs to Change.* THE Campus Learn, Share, Connect. www.timeshighereducation.com/campus/were-living-world-artificial-intelligence-its-academic-publishing-needs-change.

Moya, B., Eaton, S. E., Pethrick, H., et al. (2023). Academic integrity and artificial intelligence in higher education contexts: A rapid scoping review protocol. *Canadian Perspectives on Academic Integrity, 5*(2), Article 2.

Nachalon, Y., Broer, M., & Nativ-Zeltzer, N. (2024). Using chatGPT to generate research ideas in dysphagia: A pilot study. *Dysphagia, 39*(3), 407–411. https://doi.org/10.1007/s00455-023-10623-9.

Newman, M., & Gough, D. (2020). Systematic reviews in educational research: Methodology, perspectives and application. In O. Zawacki-Richter, M. Kerres, S. Bedenlier, M. Bond, & K. Buntins (Eds.), *Systematic Reviews in Educational Research* (pp. 3–22). Springer Fachmedien Wiesbaden. https://doi.org/10.1007/978-3-658-27602-7_1.

Nicolletti, L., & Bass, D. (2023). *Generative AI Takes Stereotypes and Bias from Bad to Worse.* Bloomberg. www.bloomberg.com/graphics/2023-generative-ai-bias/.

Nyaaba, M., Wright, A., & Choi, G. L. (2024a). *Generative AI and Digital Neocolonialism in Global Education: Towards an Equitable Framework* (No. arXiv:2406.02966). arXiv. https://doi.org/10.48550/arXiv.2406.02966.

Omena, J. J., Autuori, A., Vasconcelos, E. L., Subet, M., & Botta, M. (2024). AI methodology map: Practical and theoretical approach to engage with genAI for digital methods research. *Sociologica, 18*(2), Article 2. https://doi.org/10.6092/issn.1971-8853/19566.

OpenAI. (2018). *Improving Language Understanding with Unsupervised Learning.* https://openai.com/index/language-unsupervised/.

OpenAI. (2024). *Consumer Privacy at OpenAI.* https://openai.com/consumer-privacy/.

Ozano, K., & Khatri, R. (2018). Reflexivity, positionality and power in cross-cultural participatory action research with research assistants in rural Cambodia. *Educational Action Research, 26*(2), 190–204. https://doi.org/10.1080/09650792.2017.1331860.

Peres, R., Schreier, M., Schweidel, D., & Sorescu, A. (2023). On ChatGPT and beyond: How generative artificial intelligence may affect research, teaching, and practice. *International Journal of Research in Marketing, 40*(2), 269–275. https://doi.org/10.1016/j.ijresmar.2023.03.001.

References

Perkins, M. (2023). Academic integrity considerations of AI large language models in the post-pandemic era: ChatGPT and beyond. *Journal of University Teaching and Learning Practice*, *20*(2), Article 2. https://doi.org/10.53761/1.20.02.07.

Perkins, M., Furze, L., Roe, J., & MacVaugh, J. (2024). The Artificial Intelligence Assessment Scale (AIAS): A framework for ethical integration of generative AI in educational assessment. *Journal of University Teaching and Learning Practice*, *21*(06), Article 06. https://doi.org/10.53761/q3azde36.

Perkins, M., & Roe, J. (2024a). Academic publisher guidelines on AI usage: A ChatGPT supported thematic analysis. *F1000Research*, *12*, 1398. https://doi.org/10.12688/f1000research.142411.2.

Perkins, M., & Roe, J. (2024b). Decoding academic integrity policies: A corpus linguistics investigation of AI and other technological threats. *Higher Education Policy*, *37*(3), 633–653. https://doi.org/10.1057/s41307-023-00323-2.

Perkins, M., & Roe, J. (2024c). *Generative AI Tools in Academic Research: Applications and Implications for Qualitative and Quantitative Research Methodologies* (No. arXiv:2408.06872). arXiv. https://doi.org/10.48550/arXiv.2408.06872.

Perkins, M., & Roe, J. (2024d). The use of Generative AI in qualitative analysis: Inductive thematic analysis with ChatGPT. *Journal of Applied Learning and Teaching*, *7*(1), 390–395. https://journals.sfu.ca/jalt/index.php/jalt/article/download/1585/753/5729.

Perkins, M., Roe, J., Vu, B. H., et al. (2024). Simple techniques to bypass GenAI text detectors: Implications for inclusive education. *International Journal of Educational Technology in Higher Education*, *21*(1), 1–25. https://doi.org/10.1186/s41239-024-00487-w.

Perplexity. (2024). *What Is Perplexity?* www.perplexity.ai/hub/faq/what-is-perplexity.

Perrier, E., & Bennett, M. T. (2024). *An AI System Has Reached Human Level on a Test for 'General Intelligence': Here's What that Means*. The Conversation. http://theconversation.com/an-ai-system-has-reached-human-level-on-a-test-for-general-intelligence-heres-what-that-means-246529.

Picazo-Sanchez, P., & Ortiz-Martin, L. (2024). Analysing the impact of ChatGPT in research. *Applied Intelligence*, *54*(5), 4172–4188. https://doi.org/10.1007/s10489-024-05298-0.

Pichai, S., Hassabis, D., & Kavukcuoglu, K. (2024). *Introducing Gemini 2.0: Our New AI Model for the Agentic Era*. Google. https://blog.google/technology/google-deepmind/google-gemini-ai-update-december-2024/.

Pratschke, B. M. (2024). *Generative AI and Education: Digital Pedagogies, Teaching Innovation and Learning Design.* Springer Nature Switzerland. https://doi.org/10.1007/978-3-031-67991-9.

Radford, A. (2018). *Improving Language Understanding by Generative Pre-training.* https://hayate-lab.com/wp-content/uploads/2023/05/43372bfa750340059ad87ac8e538c53b.pdf.

Rashid, S., & Yadav, S. S. (2020). Impact of Covid-19 pandemic on higher education and research. *Indian Journal of Human Development, 14*(2), 340–343. https://doi.org/10.1177/0973703020946700.

Richter, S., Giroux, M., Piven, I., Sima, H., & Dodd, P. (2024). A constructivist approach to integrating AI in marketing education: Bridging theory and practice. *Journal of Marketing Education*, 02734753241288876. https://doi.org/10.1177/02734753241288876.

Ríos, C. de los, & Patel, L. (2023). Positions, positionality, and relationality in educational research. *International Journal of Qualitative Studies in Education.* 1–12. www.tandfonline.com/doi/abs/10.1080/09518398.2023.2268036.

Roe, J. (2025). Generative AI as cultural artifact: Applying anthropological methods to AI literacy. *Postdigital Science and Education.* https://doi.org/10.1007/s42438-025-00547-y.

Roe, J., Furze, L., & Perkins, M. (2024). *Funhouse Mirror or Echo Chamber? A Methodological Approach to Teaching Critical AI Literacy Through Metaphors* (No. arXiv:2411.14730). arXiv. https://doi.org/10.48550/arXiv.2411.14730.

Roe, J., & Perkins, M. (2022). What are automated paraphrasing tools and how do we address them? A review of a growing threat to academic integrity. *International Journal for Educational Integrity, 18*(1), 1–10. https://doi.org/10.1007/s40979-022-00109-w.

Roe, J., & Perkins, M. (2023). 'What they're not telling you about ChatGPT': Exploring the discourse of AI in UK news media headlines. *Humanities and Social Sciences Communications, 10*(1), 1–9. https://doi.org/10.1057/s41599-023-02282-w.

Roe, J., & Perkins, M. (2024a). Deepfakes and higher education: A research agenda and scoping review of synthetic media. *Journal of University Teaching and Learning Practice, 21*(10), 1–22. https://doi.org/10.53761/2y2np178.

Roe, J., & Perkins, M. (2024b). *Generative AI and Agency in Education: A Critical Scoping Review and Thematic Analysis* (No. arXiv:2411.00631). arXiv. https://doi.org/10.48550/arXiv.2411.00631.

Roe, J., & Perkins, M. (2024d). *Generative AI in Self-Directed Learning: A Scoping Review* (No. arXiv:2411.07677). arXiv. https://doi.org/10.48550/arXiv.2411.07677.

Roe, J., Perkins, M., Chonu, G. K., & Bhati, A. (2023). Student perceptions of peer cheating behaviour during COVID-19 induced online teaching and assessment. *Higher Education Research & Development*, 43(4), 966–980. https://doi.org/10.1080/07294360.2023.2258820

Roe, J., Perkins, M., Chonu, G. K., & Bhati, A. (2024). Student perceptions of peer cheating behaviour during COVID-19 induced online teaching and assessment. *Higher Education Research & Development*, *43*(4), 966–980. https://doi.org/10.1080/07294360.2023.2258820.

Roe, J., Perkins, M., & Furze, L. (2024). Deepfakes and higher education: A research agenda and scoping review of synthetic media. *Journal of University Teaching and Learning Practice*, *21*(10), 1–22.

Roe, J., Perkins, M., & Ruelle, D. (2024a). Is GenAI the future of feedback? Understanding student and staff perspectives on AI in assessment. *Intelligent Technologies in Education*. https://open-publishing.org/journals/index.php/ited/article/view/1184.

Roe, J., Renandya, W., & Jacobs, G. (2023). A review of AI-powered writing tools and their implications for academic integrity in the language classroom. *Journal of English and Applied Linguistics*, *2*(1), 22–30. https://doi.org/10.59588/2961-3094.1035.

Rudolph, J., Ismail, F. M. M., & Popenici, S. (2024). Higher education's generative artificial intelligence paradox: The meaning of chatbot mania. *Journal of University Teaching and Learning Practice*, *21*(06), Article 06. https://doi.org/10.53761/54fs5e77.

Rudolph, J., Tan, S., & Tan, S. (2023a). ChatGPT: Bullshit spewer or the end of traditional assessments in higher education? *Journal of Applied Learning and Teaching*, *6*(1), Article 1. https://doi.org/10.37074/jalt.2023.6.1.9.

Rudolph, J., Tan, S., & Tan, S. (2023b). War of the chatbots: Bard, Bing Chat, ChatGPT, Ernie and beyond. The new AI gold rush and its impact on higher education. *Journal of Applied Learning and Teaching*, *6*(1), 364–389.

Ruksakulpiwat, S., Kumar, A., & Ajibade, A. (2023). Using ChatGPT in medical research: Current status and future directions. *Journal of Multidisciplinary Healthcare*, *16*(null), 1513–1520. https://doi.org/10.2147/JMDH.S413470.

Saccenti, D., Buattini, M., Grazioli, S., & Torres, D. (2024). Navigating the AI frontier: Should we fear ChatGPT use in higher education and scientific research? Finding a middle ground through guiding principles and practical applications. *Possibility Studies & Society*, *2*(4), 415–437. https://doi.org/10.1177/27538699241231862.

Sarı, T., Nayir, F., & Bozkurt, A. (2024). Reimagining education: Bridging artificial intelligence, transhumanism, and critical pedagogy. *Journal of*

Educational Technology and Online Learning, 7(1), Article 1. https://doi.org/10.31681/jetol.1308022.

Seta, G. de, Pohjonen, M., & Knuutila, A. (2023). *Synthetic Ethnography: Field Devices for the Qualitative Study of Generative Models*. OSF. https://doi.org/10.31235/osf.io/zvew4.

Shardlow, M., & Przybyła, P. (2024). Deanthropomorphising NLP: Can a language model be conscious? *PLOS ONE, 19*(12), e0307521. https://doi.org/10.1371/journal.pone.0307521.

Sharma, M., Tong, M., Korbak, T., et al. (2023). *Towards Understanding Sycophancy in Language Models* (No. arXiv:2310.13548). arXiv. https://doi.org/10.48550/arXiv.2310.13548.

Shrivastava, R. (2024). *Garbage in, Garbage out: Perplexity Spreads Misinformation From Spammy AI Blog Posts*. Forbes. www.forbes.com/sites/rashishrivastava/2024/06/26/search-startup-perplexity-increasingly-cites-ai-generated-sources/.

Siemens, G. (2018). Connectivism. Foundations of Learning and Instructional Design Technology: Historical Roots and Current Trends. https://edtechbooks.org/lidtfoundations/connectivism.

Singh Chawla, D. (2024). Is ChatGPT corrupting peer review? Telltale words hint at AI use. *Nature, 628*(8008), 483–484. https://doi.org/10.1038/d41586-024-01051-2.

Stanistreet, P., Elfert, M., & Atchoarena, D. (2020). Education in the age of COVID-19: Understanding the consequences. *International Review of Education, 66*(5), 627–633. https://doi.org/10.1007/s11159-020-09880-9.

Strzelecki, A., Cicha, K., Rizun, M., & Rutecka, P. (2024). Acceptance and use of ChatGPT in the academic community. *Education and Information Technologies, 29*(17), 22943–22968. https://doi.org/10.1007/s10639-024-12765-1.

Suppes, P. (1974). The place of theory in educational research. *Educational Researcher, 3*(6), 3–10. https://doi.org/10.3102/0013189X003006003.

Tang, G., & Eaton, S. E. (2024). A rapid investigation of artificial intelligence generated content footprints in scholarly publications. *Journal of Scholarly Publishing, 55*(3), 337–355. https://doi.org/10.3138/jsp-2023-0079.

Tang, K.-S. (2024). Claiming the research expertise on human–GenAI interaction for sociolinguistics. *Journal of Sociolinguistics, 28*(5), 16–19. https://doi.org/10.1111/josl.12683.

TEQSA. (2022). *What Is Academic Integrity? | Tertiary Education Quality and Standards Agency*. www.teqsa.gov.au/students/understanding-academic-integrity/what-academic-integrity.

Tricco AC, et al. (2018). *PRISMA extension for scoping reviews (PRISMA-ScR): checklist and explanation*. Annals of Internal Medicine, *169*(7), 467–473.

Turner, K. L., Adams, J. D., & Eaton, S. E. (2022). Academic integrity, STEM education, and COVID-19: A call to action. *Cultural Studies of Science Education*, *17*(2), 331–339. https://doi.org/10.1007/s11422-021-10090-4.

Turobov, A., Coyle, D., & Harding, V. (2024). *Using ChatGPT for Thematic Analysis* (No. arXiv:2405.08828). arXiv. https://doi.org/10.48550/arXiv.2405.08828.

van den Berg, G., & du Plessis, E. (2023). ChatGPT and generative AI: Possibilities for its contribution to lesson planning, critical thinking and openness in teacher education. *Education Sciences*, *13*(10), Article 10. https://doi.org/10.3390/educsci13100998.

van Manen, M. (2023). What does ChatGPT mean for qualitative health research? *Qualitative Health Research*, *33*(13), 1135–1139. https://doi.org/10.1177/10497323231210816.

Vaswani, A., Shazeer, N., Parmar, N., et al. (2017). Attention is all you need. *Advances in Neural Information Processing Systems*, *30*, 1–11. https://proceedings.neurips.cc/paper_files/paper/2017/hash/3f5ee243547dee91fbd053c1c4a845aa-Abstract.html.

Vygotsky, L. (1962). *Thought and Language* (pp. xxi, 168). MIT Press. https://doi.org/10.1037/11193-000.

Wachinger, J., Bärnighausen, K., Schäfer, L. N., Scott, K., & McMahon, S. A. (2024). Prompts, pearls, imperfections: Comparing ChatGPT and a human researcher in qualitative data analysis. *Qualitative Health Research*, 10497323241244669. https://doi.org/10.1177/10497323241244669.

Wang, R.-C., Yang, D., Hsieh, M.-C., Chen, Y.-C., & Lin, W. (2024). GenAI-assisted database deployment for heterogeneous indigenous–native ethnographic research data. *Applied Sciences*, *14*(16), 7414. https://doi.org/10.3390/app14167414.

Wang, S., Wang, F., Zhu, Z., Wang, J., Tran, T., & Du, Z. (2024). Artificial intelligence in education: A systematic literature review. *Expert Systems with Applications*, *252*, 124167. https://doi.org/10.1016/j.eswa.2024.124167.

Warr M. (2024). Blending generative AI, critical pedagogy, and teacher education to expose and challenge automated inequality. In Blankenship R., Cherner T. (Eds.), *Research Highlights in Technology and Teacher Education*. AACE.

Watermeyer, R., Lanclos, D., Phipps, L., et al. (2024). Academics' weak(ening) resistance to generative AI: The cause and cost of prestige? *Postdigital Science and Education*. 1–21. https://doi.org/10.1007/s42438-024-00524-x

Weber-Wulff, D., Anohina-Naumeca, A., Bjelobaba, S., et al. (2023). Testing of detection tools for AI-generated text. *International Journal for Educational Integrity*, *19*(1), Article 1. https://doi.org/10.1007/s40979-023-00146-z.

Wei, J., Tay, Y., Bommasani, R., et al. (2022). *Emergent Abilities of Large Language Models* (No. arXiv:2206.07682). arXiv. https://doi.org/10.48550/arXiv.2206.07682.

Whitfield, S., & Hofmann, M. A. (2023). Elicit: AI literature review research assistant. *Public Services Quarterly, 19*(3), 201–207. https://doi.org/10.1080/15228959.2023.2224125.

Williams, A., Milagros, M., & Gebru, T. (2022). *The Exploited Labor behind Artificial Intelligence.* Noema. www.noemamag.com/the-exploited-labor-behind-artificial-intelligence/.

Wu, X., Duan, R., & Ni, J. (2024). Unveiling security, privacy, and ethical concerns of ChatGPT. *Journal of Information and Intelligence, 2*(2), 102–115. https://doi.org/10.1016/j.jiixd.2023.10.007.

Xu, F., Uszkoreit, H., Du, Y., et al. (2019). Explainable AI: A brief survey on history, research areas, approaches and challenges. In J. Tang, M.-Y. Kan, D. Zhao, S. Li, & H. Zan (Eds.), *Natural Language Processing and Chinese Computing* (Vol. 11839, pp. 563–574). Springer International. https://doi.org/10.1007/978-3-030-32236-6_51.

Yan, L., Echeverria, V., Fernandez-Nieto, G. M., et al. (2024). Human-AI collaboration in thematic analysis using ChatGPT: A user study and design recommendations. *Extended Abstracts of the CHI Conference on Human Factors in Computing Systems*, 1–7. https://doi.org/10.1145/3613905.3650732.

Yao, J.-Y., Ning, K.-P., Liu, Z.-H., et al. (2024). *LLM Lies: Hallucinations Are Not Bugs, but Features as Adversarial Examples* (No. arXiv:2310.01469). arXiv. https://doi.org/10.48550/arXiv.2310.01469.

Zawacki-Richter, O., Kerres, M., Bedenlier, S., Bond, M., & Buntins, K. (Eds.). (2020). *Systematic Reviews in Educational Research: Methodology, Perspectives and Application.* Springer Fachmedien. https://doi.org/10.1007/978-3-658-27602-7.

Zhang, H., Wu, C., Xie, J., et al. (2024). *Redefining Qualitative Analysis in the AI Era: Utilizing ChatGPT for Efficient Thematic Analysis* (No. arXiv:2309.10771). arXiv. https://doi.org/10.48550/arXiv.2309.10771.

Zhao, W. X., Zhou, K., Li, J., et al. (2024). *A Survey of Large Language Models* (No. arXiv:2303.18223). arXiv. https://doi.org/10.48550/arXiv.2303.18223.

Zhgenti, S., & Holmes, W. (2023). *Generative AI and Education: Adopting a Critical Approach.* https://discovery.ucl.ac.uk/id/eprint/10177781/1/Zhgenti%20and%20Holmes%20-%202023%20-%20Generative%20AI%20and%20Education%20Adopting%20a%20Critical%20A.pdf.

Cambridge Elements ≡

Research Methods in Education

Sal Consoli
University of Edinburgh

Dr Sal Consoli is an Assistant Professor in Language Education and Director of Research Methods in Education at the University of Edinburgh. He is also Research Fellow at KTH Royal Institute of Technology, Sweden and Advisory Board member of the Research Center for International and Global Higher Education at Khazar University, Azerbaijan. His research interests include the psychology of language education and internationalisation of education. His work has appeared in international journals such as *System, Higher Education, TESOL Quarterly, Language Teaching Research, RELC, Applied Linguistics Review*, and *Journal of English for Academic Purposes*. His research has been funded by the Economic and Social Research Council, the Hong Kong UGC, and the Leverhulme Trust. He has developed the concept of *life capital* for language education research, and this is now being used in various sub-domains of mainstream education. Dr Consoli has an active interest in researcher reflexivity, and he is Co-Editor of *Reflexivity in Applied Linguistics* (Routledge, 2023). He is also Associate Editor of the journal *Research Methods in Applied Linguistics* (Elsevier). He serves on the committees of several learned societies such as the British Association of Applied Linguistics and he is also a Fellow of the Royal Society of Arts (UK).

Samantha Curle
University of Bath

Samantha Curle (DPhil, FRSA, FHEA) is a Reader in Education (Applied Linguistics), Director of all MRes programmes (Faculty of Humanities and Social Sciences), and Institutional Academic Lead for the South-West Doctoral Training Partnership (SWDTP) at the University of Bath. She is also Adjunct Professor at Khazar University (Azerbaijan) and an Associate Member of the English Medium Instruction (EMI) Oxford Research Group. Dr. Curle's research interest lies in factors affecting academic achievement in EMI in higher education, such as English proficiency and psychological constructs. She has published seven edited books on EMI (three forthcoming), led a global comparative EMI report for the British Council, and her EMI-related research has been published in journals such as *Language Teaching, Applied Linguistics Review, Studies in Higher Education, Journal of Engineering Education, Journal for the Psychology of Language Learning*, and *Journal of English for Academic Purposes*. Her research spans across four continents (Africa, Asia, Europe, South America), and has been funded by the European Commission, the National Research Councils in Hong Kong, Spain and Turkey, the British Academy Newton Fund, as well as the British Council. Dr. Curle has been ranked top scholar in the world for research output on EMI by SciVal. She is also a Fellow of the Higher Education Academy and the Royal Society of Arts (UK).

About the series

The *Cambridge Elements in Research Methods in Education* series offers a ground-breaking approach to educational research, providing cutting-edge methodologies tailored to today's dynamic, multicultural, and technology-driven educational settings. Readers can expect in-depth, evidence-based guidance on specific methods designed to enhance both traditional and emerging research practices. Each *Element* will delve into a particular approach, offering readers clear, practical guidance that balances rigour with flexibility. By clustering content around key themes—such as reflexivity, digital innovation, and diverse ontological perspectives—this series offers a comprehensive toolkit that responds to the complex challenges educational researchers and students face in the contemporary research arena.

Each Element showcases cutting-edge research and builds upon established literature, while also opening new avenues for underexplored and interdisciplinary topics, from decolonising research methods to digital education. This series provides a rich resource for educational researchers, undergraduate and graduate students alike. This is with the aim of creating a platform where innovative research practices and practical solutions converge to push the boundaries of educational inquiry in a way that's accessible, adaptable, creative, and impactful.

Cambridge Elements

Research Methods in Education

Elements in the Series

How to Use Generative AI in Educational Research
Jasper Roe

A full series listing is available at: www.cambridge.org/ERME

Printed by Libri Plureos GmbH in Hamburg, Germany